$130.00

IMAGINING
THEOLOGY

IMAGINING THEOLOGY

WOMEN, WRITING AND GOD

Heather Walton

t & t clark

Published by T&T Clark International
A Continuum Imprint
The Tower Building, 11 York Road, London SE1 7NX
80 Maiden Lane, Suite 704, New York, NY 10038

www.continuumbooks.com

British Library Cataloguing-in-Publication Data
A catalogue record for this book is available from the British Library

Typeset by Free Range Book Design & Production Ltd
Printed on acid-free paper in Great Britain by Cromwell Press Ltd,
Trowbridge, Wiltshire

ISBN-13: 978-0-567-03173-0 (hardback)
ISBN-10: 0-567-03173-X (hardback)

FOR

HAZEL AND KEITH

Contents

(xҕ)

Acknowledgements

T hank you to the friends whose challenge, support and influence have so shaped my work. Particular gratitude is due to: Elaine Graham, Frances Ward, Susan Durber, Mary Coates, David Jasper, Alison Jasper and Yvonne Sherwood. My family have been a vital source of sanity and humour. Thank you Reinier, Maia, Mel and John. Thanks also to Alana Howard and Thomas Kraft for helping to bring this project to completion.

A number of the essays in this collection have been previously published in journals or edited collections. I am grateful to the following publishers for permission to reproduce them here:

To Ashgate for permission to publish 'Literature and Theology: Sex in the Relationship' in Darlene Bird and Yvonne Sherwood (eds), *Bodies in Question: Gender, Religion, Text*, 2005.

To *Contact: The Interdisciplinary Journal of Practical Theology and Pastoral Care* for permission to use parts of 'The Wisdom of Sheba: The Construction of Feminist Practical Theology', *Contact: The Interdisciplinary Journal of Pastoral Studies*, no. 135, 2001, pp. 3–12.

To Oxford University Press for permission to publish 'Extreme Faith in the Work of Elizabeth Smart and Luce Irigaray', *Literature and Theology*, vol. 16, no. 1, 2002, pp. 40–50 and extracts from 'The Feminist Literary Revisioning of Sacred Traditions' in David Jasper, Andrew Hass and Elizabeth Jay (eds), *The Oxford Handbook of Literature and Theology*, 2007.

To Sage for permission to publish 'The Gender of the Cyborg', *Theology and Sexuality*, vol. 10, no. 2, 2004, pp. 33–44 and 'Sex in the War: An Aesthetics of Resistance in the Diaries of Etty Hillesum', *Theology and Sexuality*, vol. 12, no. 1, 2005, pp. 51–61.

Preface

Preparing a collection of your own work for publication is a very salutary experience. This book brings together essays published earlier in the decade alongside articles recently in print or especially written for this text. What was not apparent to me before I made this selection, but is strikingly obvious to me now, is that I return to consider the same themes from different perspectives in all my writing. I determinedly insist on the distinctions between literature and theology in order to explore what happens when the disciplines contend with each other or, as sometimes also happens, surprise themselves in an amorous embrace. This concern to explore the erotic tension between literature and theology distinguishes my approach from that of many others working in this interdisciplinary field. I do not stress the complementarity of these subjects and seek out the places where their horizons merge and fuse. I am much more interested in the uneasy ambivalence which characterizes their relationship.

Although this is a book about the interdisciplinary study of literature and theology, its concerns are far broader than what happens when actual, 'shelveable' texts from these ancient disciplines encounter each other in an academic context. The terms literature and theology trail a wide range of associations in their wake and are frequently used heuristically to describe different means of apprehending the world. Theology is typically associated with order, authority, clarity, reason, responsibility and discernment. Literature, in contrast, is associated with excess, beauty, mystery and our embodied passions. It is also evident that the two terms represent gendered locations within our culture. I have exploited these conventions, and it is frequently the case that when I am discussing what happens when literature meets theology I am also questioning what happens when the feminine imaginary meets the male symbolic, when beauty meets ethics, when aesthetics meets politics, when the spiritual meets the material, when human bodies incarnate the divine and when human suffering cries out to God. The fact that the interdisciplinary terrain of literature and theology is a place where these big questions can be articulated and wrestled with is the major reason why I have made this uncomfortable but exhilarating borderland territory my home.

It is also the major reason why an area of scholarship that might be thought to be a minority concern is such a creative place to be located at the present time. This collection rightly belongs with the burgeoning number of publications being generated in what is a dynamic and rapidly expanding area of research. It does, however, have a distinct character and agenda. Despite the vivid and insightful contribution women have made to conversations between literature and theology, their work has not entered the mainstream of debate and has been largely ignored by male scholars. This volume both interrogates the possible causes of this margin-alization and foregrounds the work of women authors and theorists. Of course I hope that my work will contribute to bringing women's original and challenging writing into greater prominence. Even if this is not an immediately attainable goal it is possible that interventions like this will be part of a process of infection, they will effect a gradual contagion of an area of discourse that is currently male centred and resistant to exploring concerns that are frequently associated with women but are of vital concern to us all.

I hope that this might be so. It is natural to have such aspirations for a book you have just finished working on and are about to send out on its way into the world. But whatever its fortunes I have a fondness for it. It is in many ways a deeply personal text. I have been writing about women I love and I have loved writing about them. It's also been a privilege to have had the space to keep on asking the questions that fascinate me most (over and over again!) in the company of people who are willing to debate them with me. I am grateful to those friends, colleagues and students associated with the Centre for Literature, Theology and the Arts at Glasgow University who have often been the first recipients of the research papers that later became these chapters. This radical and open academic community has left its mark on all my work.

Chapter 1

What Everyone was Reading: The Uses of Literature in Feminist Theology

Heading for the book shop not the library

Feminism is a peculiarly literary movement. One of the most exciting parts of my own feminist journey was the early realization that many of the great intellectual and political pioneers of the women's movement had also been writers of fiction. I found I could curl up in bed with Mary Wollstonecraft, Alexandra Kollontai, Virginia Woolf and Simone de Beauvoir – in a way that was not possible with Lenin or pleasing with Sartre.[1] Moreover, their writings revealed that feminists could not be classed according to the dominant stereotypes of humourless, dull, dogmatic and asexual women. Their books were wild, erotic and unorthodox. Reading them, I found reassurance that what feminists wanted was a world of intense colour and it seemed to me hugely important that the textual inheritance of feminism contained so many significant works of literature.

It is not surprising that these women, who lived lives in defiance of cultural norms, should have invested their energy in creating works of fiction. Clearly it paid them and pleased them to write. But this lucrative pleasure should not be regarded as something 'removed' from their engagement in other spheres. Ricoeur, following Artistotle, has argued that imaginative writing is a space in which practical wisdom can be exercised through the creation of alternative worlds (1991: 85). In this frame there is a direct correspondence between the fictional energy of women and their

---

[1]   Who did write novels but only with grim intent.

political activism. Indeed writing itself takes on the role of destabilizing a world of established meanings. But not only writing. Reading literature has similar subversive potential as the reader brings her own contribution to this imaginative work.

And feminism *is* a peculiarly literary movement. The feminist 'public sphere', in which the conversational activity that characterizes dynamic political movements takes place, has been characterized as a reading community. In this arena works of fiction have played an enormous role in both introducing women to feminist ideas and inspiring processes of personal and social transformation (see Lauret 1994).

So a passion for reading has characterized the development of feminist consciousness and the second wave of the movement, as it has developed from the 1960s onwards, can claim to have not only constituted an avid reading public but also generated an unofficial canon of classic feminist texts. Furthermore, feminist literary criticism has developed with corresponding energy and through its scholarship women have rediscovered many forgotten literary treasures, learned to critique what is celebrated as good literature and asked questions about what it means to read and write 'as a woman'.

Religious feminists have participated enthusiastically in most aspects of this literary activity and in this chapter I shall argue that it is possible to chart broad epochs in the development of feminist theology in relation to the literature women were reading and referring to in their theological writings. This thesis could be stated even more strongly. I think it is impossible fully to comprehend the development of feminist theology without asking what women were reading in bed, on the bus and in their book groups. The argument might also be taken a stage further. If an examination of the literary milieu in which feminist theology has been formed can be interesting and illuminating, should it not be possible to discern some future directions from current reading practices?

In this chapter I will discuss some of the key works which have influenced the trajectory of feminist theology during the past three decades. However, before beginning this examination it is interesting to note that feminist theologians have not demonstrated great interest in the literary critical activities of secular feminists. Although, as I have argued elsewhere (Walton 2007), women's literature abounds in vivid and unorthodox namings of the divine, it has largely been left to literary scholars to unearth and claim these treasures and feminist theologians have shown only a passing, strategic interest in this endeavour.[2] There is a huge, and largely unexplored, hinterland that lies behind the current use of literature in feminist theology but we have not been heading for the library to

---

[2]   This is particularly interesting as the reclamation of forgotten textual sources has been so hugely significant in other areas of feminist theological scholarship such as biblical studies and church history.

research this but rather to the bookshops where new writing is displayed. It is popular, in the sense of best-selling, contemporary works of fiction that have been our chief resource. We have been substantially shaped by 'what everyone was reading'.

The 1970s: everyone was reading Doris Lessing

And this is not surprising. Virginia Woolf commented hilariously on the frustrations women have faced in searching for their identity amongst the index cards of the library catalogue. She found them to be both invisible in the fullness of their personhood and endlessly dissected into the very peculiar and particular categories constructed by male scholars. She was also famously denied admission to the prestigious resources of the academy in a way that initially caused her grief and anger but later encouraged her to muse that it might be better to be locked out of the library than locked in (1977 [1929]: 29).

Women seeking self-understanding a generation after Woolf found themselves in a very similar position. Whilst they might have gained freer access to the library shelves, they continued to be constrained by curricula and 'reading lists' constructed by men in which the works and concerns of women were largely ignored. There were very few women scholars writing about the lives of women whose works were considered academically credible enough to merit serious attention. Outstanding amongst these were Simone de Beauvoir (in her academic gown) and Margaret Mead. Their writings were pored over and endlessly re-cited by women students eager to construct a base upon which they could begin to articulate their own perspectives. However, it was difficult to raise an alternative epistemological platform upon such slender foundations. Fortunately outside the academy developments were taking place which were to propel feminist thinking into a new era. The fiction of Doris Lessing played an important role in these and her work became hugely influential within the developing feminist movement. Elaine Showalter paid this early tribute to her contribution:

> She has an extraordinary, barometric sensitivity to the social climate, but she anticipates trends rather than capping them with a novel. Thus the encyclopaedic study of intellectual, political women in *The Golden Notebook* preceded and in a sense introduced the Women's Liberation Movement. (1979: 307)

Showalter's assessment of Lessing's role as both mirror and model for women in the late 1960s and early 70s is confirmed by later scholars. Greene, for example, describes her writing as having an unprecedented impact (1991: 106) that was startling at the time and is difficult to comprehend in the changed circumstances of today. Her books were both revelatory and shocking; not because she described situations which were unfamiliar to her women readers but rather because they read within them their own concerns set down in print for the first time. Lessing, credited with authoring the first tampon in English literature, spoke powerfully to an emerging constituency of feminist activists who found her descriptions of clever women, with politics and periods, reflective of their own experience in an era of massive social transition. In this famous extract from *The Golden Notebook* (1973) Lessing's narrator reflects on how difficult it is to break the silence concerning women's lives. Having set herself the exercise of recording all her feelings during the course of a day, she is thrown into doubt about the worth of this effort when she notices blood on her bedsheets:

> As I push the stained sheet into the linen-basket I notice a stain of blood. But surely it is not time yet for my period. I check my dates, and realize yes, it's today. ... (I wondered whether it would be better not to choose today to write down everything I felt; then decided to go ahead. It was not planned; I had forgotten about the period. I decided that the instinctive feeling of shame and modesty was dishonest: no emotion for a writer.) I stuff my vagina with the tampon of cotton wool, and am already on my way downstairs, when I remember I've forgotten to take a supply of tampons with me. I am late ... I am worrying about this business of being conscious of everything so as to write it down particularly in connection with my having a period ... I know that as soon as I write down the word blood it will have the wrong emphasis, and even to me when I come to read what I have written. And so I begin to doubt the value of a day of recording without having begun to record it. (1973: 334–5)

Through the device of 'writing-about-writing-about' intimate experience Lessing offers a compelling image in print of the dichotomy many women felt existed between their lived experience and what it was acceptable to speak about in public. This tension set the agenda of the consciousness-raising groups that began to proliferate in the late 1960s and in which women began to address their perceptions of confinement and cultural invisibility. A sense of dissonance was named in relation to many spheres of life but for the few women seeking recognition within theological circles the feelings of alienation and isolation were painfully intense.

Two of the most influential foremothers of contemporary religious feminism, Carol Christ and Judith Plaskow, were students at Yale during this period. Here they noted the complete absence of awareness of issues relating to women in every branch of theological study. In the militant spirit of the times they made every effort to address this situation through their own research but were met with hostility and ridicule from their professors and fellow students:

We remember the day we proposed to a professor that we might take one of our comprehensives on the history of Christian attitudes towards women. Although we were armed with seven or eight pages of sources on the subject we had no sooner mentioned the topic than he slammed his fist down on the table and shouted 'not for me, you're not!' We also remember Carol's turning in a seminar paper on Barth's view of women to a professor who glanced at the title and remarked that he had never considered *that* a very important topic. He then went on to discuss the papers presented by the males in the class. (1979a: ix)

Fortunately Christ and Plaskow were undeterred by these rebuffs and determined to do all they could to call the discipline to account for its exclusion of women's voices. In common with women in other spheres they found that the academic resources to accomplish this task were depressingly scarce. Valerie Saiving had published what is commonly regarded as the first essay in feminist theology in 1960 (Saiving 1979 [1960]). In common with women from other disciplines she drew upon the work of established scholars, particularly Margaret Mead, to justify her contention that there were fundamental differences between male and female experience. Her argument was that the grammar of theology was predicated 'upon the basis of masculine experience and thus views the human condition from a male standpoint. Consequently these doctrines do not provide an adequate interpretation of the situation of women' (1979 [1960] : 27).

When Christ and Plaskow encountered the writing of Lessing for the first time they discovered the means to move forward from the critical position Saiving had articulated into a more constructive phase. They did this by arguing that women's experience was now finding its fullest articulation in literary form and that literature could thus be trusted as an alternative source of knowledge that in no way required the legitimization of the academy. They believed that literature also had the potential to carry women's thinking far beyond what even feminist scholarship had yet achieved. Plaskow wrote, 'we find Simone de Beauvoir's account of womanhood deepened and affirmed by recent literature by and about women' (1980: 34). Christ similarly affirmed, 'Lessing's vision is useful precisely because it represents *women's experience* in our time' (1979 [1975]: 232, emphasis added).

It is impossible to overstate how significant Christ and Plaskow's strategic use 'women's experience', accessed through literature, was in the early development of feminist theology. It freed them from the necessity to establish an acceptable academic genealogy for their thinking and provided them with an alterative textual source of spiritual authority. Nowhere else in Western culture was women's experience 'written' and what was unmarked by scripture and tradition was voiced here. The 'discovery' of this new resource could be used to fracture the monological discourse of theology and create a legitimate ground from which to speak a new word. Some twenty years later Kathleen Sands commented that this move effected a seismic shift in theological thinking. It constituted a refusal 'to assimilate women's stories to the doctrines of men ... [and] established women's literature as a theological source that while still largely ignored by androcentric religious studies has become vital to most religious feminists' (1994: 124).

Christ and Plaskow spent many hours talking about the impact reading Lessing was making upon them. Her five-volume series *Children of Violence* and its hero Martha Quest seemed to portray perfectly the social and spiritual journey they themselves were undertaking; Christ wrote that she was so possessed by this writing that she dreamed about it for weeks (1979: 231). However, their responses to the text were markedly different. Each wrote a significant book on the basis of their encounter and we can see these as typifying two emergent approaches to feminist theology which remain important today.

Her reading of Lessing had two major implications for Carol Christ. The first was that women no longer had any need to read themselves into male texts. Women's experience, she stated, 'has not funded the sacred stories of biblical tradition ... We will no longer be content to read ourselves into stories in which the daughters do not exist' (1979: 230). Women could discover their own rich source of spiritual sustenance in literature and through 'devouring' these texts and distilling their wisdom could create their own sacred traditions.

Second, Christ came to believe, Lessing's work contained the implicit 'structure of a quest myth from the perspective of women's experience, which strikes a chord with many women' (1979: 238). This is the theme of Christ's best-known work, a feminist classic, *Diving Deep and Surfacing: Women on the Spiritual Quest* (1980). In this she explores the contours of women's spiritual quest as a journey from 'nothingness' to 'new naming' which is attested to in the work of many female authors. The substitution of women's stories for patriarchal narratives and the call for women to pursue an autonomous voyage away from the place of their negation to sites of new naming is a description of the journey Christ herself was undertaking out of male-centred traditions and towards the Goddess, a path many other religious feminists were to trace in the years which followed.

Judith Plaskow also produced a groundbreaking work, *Sex, Sin and Grace* (1980) out of her encounter with Lessing. However, in this text she is not concerned to repudiate or abandon the religious heritage out of which she has been formed. She seeks rather to enrich and diversify it through the inclusion of women's voices. She maintained, more cautiously than Christ, that 'the submerged aspect of women's experience, precisely in its particularity, has the power to direct our attention to the previously ignored aspects of human experience' (1980: 175) which have the potential to enrich theological thinking. A second trajectory in feminist theological thinking can be seen opening up here, a strategy which does not seek to replace the sacred tradition with literature but rather to create an ongoing conversation in which literature plays a role in restoring voice to women. Plaskow draws upon the Jewish tradition of Midrash to support her vision of a religious tradition that flourishes as more and more interpretations and revisions, stories about stories, are constructed around sacred texts. She writes that:

> The open-ended process of creating midrash, simultaneously serious and playful, imaginative and metaphoric, has easily lent itself to feminist use. While feminist midrash – like all midrash – is a reflection of contemporary beliefs and experiences, its root conviction is utterly traditional. It stands on the rabbinic insistence that the Bible can be made to speak to the present day. (1989: 46)

Having briefly demonstrated how important literature was to the development of two different trajectories within feminist theology I now turn to the rather different years of the 1980s when everyone was reading *The Color Purple*. And I was one of those readers …

The 1980s: everyone was reading *The Color Purple*

I vividly remember a warm summer day in the mid 1980s. I had just started my first proper job and had arranged to meet my friend Carola during my lunch break. We sat on the grass in the sunshine. Carola was cool and had brought pakora to eat while I had only an egg sandwich. She was someone whose tastes and opinions often seemed more adventurous and advanced than my own. As she invited me to share her food she also offered me some advice. 'You must read *The Color Purple*,' she said. 'Everything I believe about God and about myself is in that book.'

This novel, which everyone was reading, is justly celebrated in its own right. However, it has also come to represent a remarkable cultural awakening that was taking place in black women's writing in the 1980s. Its author, Alice Walker, not only wrote fiction. She also wrote essays in which she traced the defining elements of an emerging tradition which drew upon the historical creativity of black women in the past as a resource upon which to build for the future (see Walker 1984). Walker heralded a movement, in literature and beyond, in which black women were defining themselves in relation to each other, to their own communal identity and in contradiction to white women. She named this 'womanism' and offered the following definition of the term:

'Womanist' 1. From womanish (opp. of 'girlish' i.e., frivolous, irrespon-
sible, not serious). A black feminist or feminist of color ...
2. Also: A woman who loves other women, sexually and/or nonsexually.
Appreciates and prefers women's culture ...
3. Loves music. Loves Dance. Loves the moon. Loves the Spirit. Loves love
and food and roundness. Loves struggle. Loves the folk. Loves herself.
Regardless.
4. Womanist is to feminist as purple to lavender. (1984: xi)

An immediately striking aspect of this definition is that womanist writers
like Walker were not defining themselves on the basis of the oppression
they had suffered at the hands of whites but rather in relation to the
creative genius of their own people. Walker took as her most significant
role model the novelist, anthropologist and performer, Zorah Neale
Hurston (1891?–1960) – known as the poet of the black South. Hurston
had a wild career in many creative spheres before eventually settling in a
small black southern town that turned on its own axis having little
contact with the world outside. Her novels are concerned with the specific
dynamics of black culture and use the language, idioms and folk beliefs
of southern black people. In a moving testament Walker describes her
quest to locate Hurston's grave and raise her own monument upon it
(1984: 93–116). This gesture symbolizes her self-identification with a
tradition Hurston is seen as embodying, and other black women writers
like Cade Banbara, Maya Angelou and Toni Morrison also acknowledged
their identification with this literary inheritance.

It also generated a very significant theological response. In her famous
work *Black Womanist Ethics* (1988) Katie Cannon argues that this
literary movement, this *women's tradition*, is faithful to its cultural roots
and offers 'the sharpest available view of the Black Community's soul'
(1988: 291). Cannon's thesis is that the discourse of Christian ethics has
been predicated upon the experience of dominant groups:

> Dominant ethics ... assumes that a moral agent is free and self-directing
> ... In the black community, qualities that determine desirable ethical
> values and sound moral conduct must always take into account the
> circumstances, paradoxes and dilemmas that constrict blacks to the lowest
> rungs of the social, political and economic hierarchy. Black existence is
> deliberately and openly controlled. (1988: 283)

What black women writers have achieved is the demonstration that a
strong spiritual and ethical dimension continues to inform lives that are
lived in circumstances of immense suffering and constraint:

> black women writers authenticate in an economy of expression how
> black people creatively strain against the external limits of their lives,

how they affirm their humanity by inverting assumptions, and how they balance the continual struggles and interplay of paradoxes. (1988: 174)

Literature is an invaluable resource for Cannon because it bears testimony to the spiritual depth and resilience of black people. Cannon thus argued that the work of Hurston, and the contemporary women writers who claim her inheritance, should be acknowledged as a theological resource within the black community. To an extent that is much less evident in the fiction of white feminists,[3] black women's writing contains explicit theological reflections and Cannon herself reads this literature as a form of 'theopoesis'. The fearless articulation of spiritual ideas within black women's writing which Cannon so admired was, however, to provoke considerable controversy between womanists and feminists.

At the heart of *The Color Purple* lies a famous dialogue between the narrator, Celie, and her mentor, Shug, concerning the nature of God:

Shug a beautiful something let me tell you. She frown a little, look out across the yard, lean back in her chair, look like a big rose.

She say, my first step away from the old white man was trees. Then air. Then birds. Then other people. But one day when I was sitting quiet and feeling like a motherless child, which I was, it come to me: that feeling of being part of everything, not separate at all. I knew that if I cut a tree my arm would bleed. And I laughed and I cried and I run all around the house. I knew just what it was. In fact, when it happen, you can't miss it. It sort of like you know what, she say, grinning and rubbing high up on my thigh.

Shug! I say.

Oh, she say. God love all them feelings. That's some of the best stuff God did. (1983: 166–7)

In the introduction to their edited collection, *Weaving the Visions* (1989), Christ and Plaskow reviewed developments which had taken place in feminist theology in the 1980s. They commented upon the huge popularity of *The Color Purple* and the fact that Shug's speeches had attained almost creedal status for many religious feminists. This, for them, indicated the health of the movement. If black women were writing passages such as these then the feminist theological project could not be dismissed as representing the trivial concerns of white middle-class women in academic employment: 'That Shug and Celie's dialogue in Alice Walker's *The Color Purple* is one of the most widely quoted theological texts indicates that feminist theology is not defined by what happens in the academy' (Christ and Plaskow 1989: 5).

---

[3]   Although it is interesting that it was the mystical dimensions of Lessing's work in *Children of Violence* that was originally so inspiring to Christ.

Although, as I have shown, the concept of women's experience had been immensely significant in providing the impetus for the development of feminist theology, Christ had already laid herself open to the charge of essentializing and universalizing the concept in a manner that denied the significance of differences between women.[4] Other white feminists also appeared keen to appropriate black women's writing for their own ends. For example, in *Pure Lust* Mary Daly greets Shug and Celie as 'crones' and 'nagnostic' philosophers whose wisdom can be easily accommodated in Daly's radical rewriting of philosophy (1984: 339–404). She states that the characters and plot of the novel are 'utterly cone identified' (1984: 403). The assumption that black women's insights could be interpreted in categories, however creative, established by white women drew an increasingly critical response from black feminists angry about 'the steady stream of rhetoric aimed at convincing black women how much alike their experiences are to those of our stepsisters (Hines, in Thistlethwaite 1989: 58).

The acrimonious debate concerning the significance of 'difference' that continued through most of the 1980s and into the 90s has been well documented. In my opinion the 'loss of innocence' that it represented for feminism was both necessary and ultimately beneficial. But before moving on from here it is important to note that not all white feminists sought to annex black women's writing to their own theological territory in the manner described above. At the end of the decade Susan Thistlethwaite published *Sex, Race and God* (1989) as testimony to the theological transformations that reading black women's literature had provoked within her. The literature enabled her to acknowledge the racism that had been an important part of her cultural formation. Further it de-legitimized for her significant theological presuppositions generally regarded as 'orthodox' within feminist theology. White women were affirming a benevolent 'maternal' divine, the goodness of creation and the connectedness of women to each other. Black women's writing revealed the ambiguity of motherhood, the chaos and terror of nature and alienation as well as connectedness. Although Thistlethwaite did not repudiate feminist theological thinking she recognized it had been over-optimistically naïve and required critical reappraisal. For example, the concept of connectedness would need to be reframed:

True the connections are significant ... [but] these connections may be like flint on tinder – they produce sparks of creativity that have been kindled by conflict. But let me not coin too romantic an image that

---

4   Commenting upon Ntozake Shange's choreopoem, *For colored girls who have considered suicide/ when the rainbow is enuf* (1986 [1975]), she advised that it should be read as 'in this case women' rather than as speaking directly to black women (1980: 116).

evokes the safety of fire hearths. These sparks that fly when the connections are made by facing the terror of real conflict can burn and they can hurt. (1989: 91)[5]

Thistlethwaite's work is indicative of a new mood within religious feminism which was to enter the 1990s in a more chastened form. This was also represented in the type of literature that resourced women's theological thinking in the 90s, a decade haunted by Toni Morrison's novel *Beloved*.

The 1990s: everyone was reading *Beloved*

What quote can be given from *Beloved* (Morrison 1987), the terrible story of a mother who kills her daughter rather than see her returned to slavery? Perhaps this brief one: 'This is not a story to pass on' (1987: 275).

In *Escape from Paradise* (1994) Kathleen Sands reflects that *Beloved* contains the deepest possible acknowledgement of humanity's lost innocence. White readers are made to view their own guilt without cure and acknowledge they cannot seek salvation here. Black readers are also compelled to look on a petrifying image. The mother who gave life must choose how to end it. Through choosing to kill her child Seth's remaining days are soaked with blood (1994: 140–2).

Whilst *The Color Purple* is at heart an optimistic text that appears to sit well with the progressive aspirations of feminism and womanism there can be no doubt about the tragic nature of *Beloved*. In the 1990s the political landscape began to appear increasingly complex and women's movements were deeply affected by a widespread loss of faith in emancipatory idealism. In this climate a number of white religious feminists turned to literature precisely because its open and ambiguous form allowed them to reflect upon the intransigence of human suffering and the challenges this poses to theological certainty. For example, Sands (quoted above) argued that an encounter with the tragic represented in novels like *Beloved* was beginning to tear the fabric of theology, including feminist theology, apart. 'As a theological heuristic, the tragic highlights elemental conflicts as *questionworthy* holding open the telling wounds of absurdity and fault rather than closing them with preemptive appeals to faith' (1994: 11). 'Tragedy undermines the dominant discourse dispossessing us "of the logos of Theo"' (1994: 2). We are left to face our own

---

I read Thistlethwaite's work as a real attempt to enter into a different 'reading' relationship with black women's writing. However, not all critics have seen it in this way. Annelies van Heijst, for example, views Thistlethwaite as a more sophisticated exploiter of black women's work for her own ends than her predecessors and accuses her of appropriating the work of Cannon in particular. See van Heijst (1995: 274).

mortality, the precariousness of existence and the reality of loss. In what Sands terms our 'post age' there is no hope to be found in evading the tragic. Rather the theologian discovers her true role in attending to the experiences of those who suffer and resist even when it is not apparent how they shall overcome:

> Immersed in a living community and participating critically in its vital functions a theology more sensitive to the tragic might begin to speak in a way that crosses more worlds, searching for what is absent we may begin to discern the sites where a healing disturbance gathers to re-emerge. (1994: 16)

Women's writing, for Sands, is not a transparent window through which to view authentic experience, nor is it a convenient point from which to launch a familiar critique of male domination. Rather it offers provisional insights into the ways in which women from diverse backgrounds knot together circumstances into provisional knowledge and generate their own identity *through* this process. She reads literary texts as sites where meaning is precariously negotiated and invented:

> In that spirit I turn to literature by women, though without presuming that other women's stories are in fact my stories. My model, rather, is one of dialogue with these novels putting my stories next to theirs … For it is a task of religious feminists to inquire what this has meant and what this might be made to mean. (1994: 138)

We see in the work of Sands the emergence of a more dialogical engagement with literature. Her aims are provisional and non-hegemonic. There is no benign view of women, no stages on the quest, rather an attempt at engagement with the other in the uncertain twilight of our times. In the 1990s religious feminists from other cultural groups were also engaging with literature in a similarly ambivalent and postmodern frame. Rita Nakashima Brock (1993), for example, uses writing by Asian American women to reflect upon how they fashion a spirituality for survival out of their own cultural resources. Unlike Cannon, who found black women's writing served as a mirror to the goodness of the soul of her community, Brock paints a picture of both light and shade. For her women's fiction presents the complex ambivalence of Asian culture and the way it has mutated in connection with Western values into new and hybrid forms. It demonstrates the inadequacy of innocence (which is rejected because it has no survival value and is not empowering; 1993: 65) and the need to acknowledge multiple perspectives that generate a complex sense of self 'that is passed on through communities of meaning and accountability'. Brock writes:

A story provides resonances for understanding the ambiguities and struggles of our own lives, allowing us to see our lives more fully and honestly. These resonances are reduced when we search for guidelines for our behaviour or for clear unequivocal messages ... In the constantly shifting power structures and contexts of patriarchal societies it is up to each of us to break new ground. We must each of us, in the chaos of the postmodern age, find ways to assess the past critically and to take responsibility for our lives which have their own distinctive characters. (1993: 73)

There is an interesting similarity between the Asian American literature Brock reflects upon and black women's writing as represented by *Beloved*. Whereas Carol Christ had demanded a move away from fantasy into realism, stating that today's feminist readers require authors to 'write stories in which the spiritual and social quest can be combined in the life of a realistic woman' (Christ 1980: 40), we now see a fascination with texts in which ghosts and ancestors are becoming increasingly important tropes. These spectral presences disrupt everyday 'realistic' lives making manifest what is lost (the child, the mother, the community, God). *Beloved* speaks powerfully of an 'absent presence' evoked in literature which becomes a channel through which the dead can speak.

So in the 90s we see religious feminists opening themselves to reflection upon painful and haunted texts which display processes of mutation necessary for survival. Visions of emancipation lie beyond the horizon but the necessity of struggle and a fragile solidarity endure. These texts transgress the boundaries between guilt and innocence, faith and the absence of God and even between the living and the dead. They may appear to lack the moral certainty of former times and represent a placing of ancestral divinities and household gods alongside higher powers. The theological challenge they present is to recognize the divine in situations of impurity, ambiguity and constraint. This is the world in which we live but its ambiguity has been banished from theological reflection in the past.

Reading now

What are religious feminists reading today? This is a difficult question to answer without the benefit of hindsight! However, I have suggested that we can trace an emerging trajectory in the way religious feminists have engaged with literature: literature has had different functions, different uses, in each decade. First we see literature functioning as the voice of women's sacred experience. Second it is used as a means of countering essentializing and universal tendencies through the affirmation of difference in order that the specificity of cultural location can be accorded revelatory status. Later literature is read as challenging monological theological discourse with the claims of a suffering, impure, hybrid and haunted world. While I should stress that later reading strategies do not necessarily invalidate or supersede earlier ones, what this trajectory reveals is that feminist politics, feminist spirituality and women's literature are deeply intertwined – the politics usually informing, to a large extent, the theological agenda and directing the choice of reading. When Christ and Plaskow 'discovered' Lessing they were reading what everyone else was reading.

That the political agenda has taken the lead probably accounts for the fact that in the last thirty years religious feminists of many different persuasions have been reading *the same* literature and reflecting upon it according to their location as Christians, post Christian, goddess feminists etc. If things were to continue in the future as they have done in the past we could hazard some reasonable predictions about the reading habits of religious feminists in this decade. For example, I would guess that today's diverse movement would generate greater diversity in literary choices. I would expect that ecofeminists would draw upon the lively traditions of romanticism with its sacralization of nature (see, for example Mary Grey's use of the work of Annie Dillard in *Sacred Longings* 2003). I would imagine that religious feminists espousing materialist understandings of human society and rooted in emancipatory politics would look to the resources of popular culture and science fiction (see Elaine Graham's *Representations of the Post/human*, 2002). A turn to queer theory might result in a new interest in the work of male writers who have been hitherto ignored and women might begin to venture out of their reading ghetto.[6] Whatever happens, literature exploring ethnic, cultural or national identities will undoubtedly remain hugely significant in our deeply divided world. In this still largely imagined context it would not matter very much whether the religious reader was a goddess feminist or Jewish: the literature would be taken up and transformed within her tradition. And this may continue to be the case. Or it might not.

What has been remarkable up till now is how, despite their many differences, religious feminists of widely differing persuasions have sustained the form of a coherent movement. We have participated in the same grassroots organizations, written for shared academic journals, contributed to cooperatively organized conferences, sustained first-name communities – and, of course, read the same literature in similar ways. However, there are now signs that this noisy, disputatious body of women may no longer be able to remain in mutual conversation in the same way as it did in the past. There are many examples of tensions emerging along political fault lines. Some are now beginning to talk openly for the first time about the spectre that is haunting the girl's academy. The fact

---

[6]   See the next chapter for a fuller discussion of this subject.

is that many women previously self-identified as religious feminists now question the rhetoric of social liberation, solidarity, identity and struggle that bound us all together in the past. This is a new phenomenon for us and should be distinguished from the situation in the 90s when an awareness of the problems of universalizing approaches to politics provoked recognition of the need for provisionality and pluralism in the political arena. We are now seeing some women contemplating repentance for their belief in the feminist vision of a new heaven and a new earth and arguing that true faith should find its hope elsewhere.

As representative of this position I take the work of Susan Parsons as found in the introduction to her edited collection *The Cambridge Companion to Feminist Theology* (2002) and in her own essay 'Feminist Theology as Dogmatic Theology' (2002b: 114–34). In this she critiques the whole developmental arc of feminist theology as it originated through the affirmation of experience and has been sustained through a politics of social transformation. Parsons affirms the challenge of postmodernism to visions of reformed human societies and poststructuralist theory to notions of female identity. These discursive strategies are frequently employed by those who wish to critique liberal, enlightenment values and they function as very effective weapons. Parsons paints a persuasive picture of feminist theologians facing the collapse of their theological house of cards:

> What is thought-provoking for the theologian is the way in which feminist theology has represented, on behalf of women, the expectation of modern secular reforms that divine providence could be taken into human hands, and this, in the context of a universe believed to be without God. It has required, for this undertaking, a cluster of assumptions regarding identity, agency, history and nature to name but a few, that are themselves both unstable and philosophically questionable, and that have become more obviously and bewilderingly so in the time called Postmodernity. (2002a: xv)

> Now the language of empowerment has become a cliché for everything from shoes to electricity and the nostalgia for lost opportunities to make a better world is exploited as a style that has no more credit than a change of clothes. Such is the evidence not of a loss of faith in utopian politics but the very outworking of its logic. (2002b: 128–9)

In common with many others who pursue this line of argument Parsons is not advocating that we abandon our old commitments to enlightenment ideals for a new uncertainty but rather that we seek surer foundations in a return to orthodoxy. Our mistake has been to look to our own resources rather than to God. Christian feminist theologians (we are no longer hanging out with the other girls any more) should adopt the pose of fierce madonnas – waiting in faith and hope for the coming of God amongst us.

It would require another essay to respond fully to the challenges Parsons makes. To summarize my own position, however, I do not concede either the intellectual or practical atheism of feminist theology which Parsons views as demonstrated by the feminist 'turn into the world' (2002b: 129). I would see this turn as God-provoked[7] and vitally enriching for theology. Nor do I think that God has been absent from this noisy, diverse, awkward, embarrassing, *un*orthodox company of women who have travelled together for the past thirty years. I am grateful for the journey and also for the place where we now find ourselves. A place of ambiguity, impurity and danger – where those who do theology are not virgins.

What I think that Parsons has correctly identified, however, is the need for feminist theology to recognize its own limited vision and the fact that it constantly requires the challenge of what is other to itself in order to be healthy – or indeed to be theology at all. This 'other' can certainly be encountered within and through the revelation enshrined in ancient religious systems. However, Parsons' critique of self-reflexivity within feminist theology and her call for a return to doctrinal orthodoxy deflect attention away from the problems that still lie at the doctrinal heart of male-centred religious traditions; feminists cannot simply return home again and expect to find a welcome and a safe place to stay. To be sure vital resources for our future do lie within these traditions but they must continually be brought into tension, conflict, dialogue and vital relation with another realm that they cannot comprehend or contain. You could call this realm literature but it does have other names. And when religious feminists open themselves to literature it is a political act that is also a leap of faith.

Or can be. The subtitle of this chapter is 'The Uses of Literature in Feminist Theology'. Just as we can seek self-affirmation and security in the arms of orthodoxy so we can also seek in literature a world and a God made in our own image. I have shown just how useful literature has been for religious feminists but also argued that it has carried us into painful areas where we have had to confront difficult issues. So in these days whatever we read we should struggle to avoid what Annelies van Heijst has termed 'reading for recognition' of our own core values and concerns

---

[7] This is not to imply that all who self-identify as religious feminists are theological realists. As Beverley Clack argues in a recent article, what theological realism implies within feminist theology is not easy to define (2005). However, the fact that there are hugely diverse understandings of the divine does not correlate with a turn from God and nor is it evidence of a belief that human fulfilment is the work of our own hands alone. Much more nuanced positions than Parsons acknowledges are taken by the great majority of feminist theologians.

(1995: 256). Looking to the future and dreaming a little, I would like feminists to read dirty and dangerous texts, books that make them laugh, poems that don't rhyme and even works by men. Our reading will be a process of opening our feminist religious traditions to unexpected and possibly dark epiphanies. But what begins in mystery always ends in politics. And personally I am looking for the return of politics rather than the return of God.

Chapter 2

Reading Gaols and Women's Prisons: Interdisciplinary Politics in Literature and Theology

In the previous chapter I showed how important reading literary texts has been in the development of feminist theology. In the next chapter I shall argue that literature plays a very significant (and gendered) role in some of the most important theological debates of our time. Both chapters are primarily concerned with the way in which literature is incorporated into theological discourse and to what ends. However, in this chapter, which falls 'in between', I shall explore the liminal field of inter-disciplinary study. This is often characterized as a liberated zone of dynamic scholarship, beyond the confining structures of traditional academic disciplines. I am always uneasy about optimistic assumptions such as these. A hermeneutics of suspicion informs my own approach to interdisciplinarity. I expect to find fields of interdisciplinary study crossed by the same power lines that run just below the surface of all academic endeavours. I am particularly interested in the ways that these subter-ranean currents can reanimate gender-based conventions in a space where one might expect a new freedom from the confines of disciplinary regimes.

The concealed reality of interdisciplinarity

In the conclusion to her *Interdisciplinarity: History, Theory and Practice* (1990), which still constitutes one of the most comprehensive analyses of interdisciplinary processes yet undertaken, Julie Thompson Klein calls upon those whose work lies in interdisciplinary scholarship to become self-reflexive practitioners and begin to analyse what is actually taking place within their own particular research fields. Specifically, she calls upon them to compile narratives and histories which disclose the 'concealed reality of interdisciplinarity' (1990: 195) as it is played out in the everyday world of career paths, projects, organizations, institutions, conferences and journals. It is her expectation that when the lived dynamics of inter-disciplinary dialogue are subjected to empirical scrutiny (and this is still a surprisingly under-researched terrain) a picture will emerge of creative intellectual breakthroughs *and* unacknowledged problems, frustrations and disappointments. Furthermore, whilst practitioners will have many common experiences to share, she predicts that views of interdisciplinarity will vary according to the location of the researcher; those working on the boundaries of differing disciplines will have very differing stories to tell.

With these considerations in mind, I shall present a perspective on inter-disciplinary work in literature and theology that represents *both* an empirical analysis *and* an insider's story. I have assessed indicators of current concerns within interdisciplinary scholarship in literature and theology and used my own experience to interpret these findings.

Narratives of interdisciplinarity

Before proceeding further it is important to establish a framework for this discussion and to acknowledge that interdisciplinarity is itself something of an 'interdisciplinary topic'. It has been debated and interpreted from a wide variety of perspectives, and its story has been told in a number of different ways. Rather than selecting between these accounts, I prefer to acknowledge their continuing significance to debates within literature and theology.

One influential narrative of interdisciplinarity locates its development in the reforming and progressive humanism which flourished in some social and political environments in the post-war years and enjoyed a remarkable 'flowering' in the 1960s and 70s.[1] In these sectors efforts to achieve social advancements, or solve the problems of disease, poverty and regional inequality, were regarded as appropriately cooperative ventures requiring the participation of the finest intellects and the sharing of resources previously allocated independently. National, intergovern-mental and international agencies sponsored many such new initiatives creating new financial incentives and prestige for interdisciplinary research. From a similar ideological perspective came the view that inter-

---

[1]   Although, in fact, there had been many efforts to promote interdisciplinary conversations prior to this period (see Klein 1990: 21–3). Interdisciplinary research was important within scientific research from the 1930s and was integral to the 'war effort' and fascist experiments in 'social reconstruction'.

disciplinary education was required in order to nurture the responsible, creative and problem-solving citizens who would inhabit the projected new world order. The proponents of this view envisioned a pedagogical strategy that respected the naturally integrative nature of human development and was thus, straightforwardly, the 'best' way to teach and to learn. Rather later, but with similar intent, forms of interdisciplinary care were advocated and developed based, once again, upon holistic understandings of the nature of human wellbeing. All these forms of interdisciplinarity were practical, problem solving and pragmatic. Their aims were strategic in the first instance, but they also carried with them a particular anthropology. In this frame, interdisciplinarity springs directly from the essential nature of the human being and the human quest to create a better world.

If this first narrative of interdisciplinarity is optimistic there is a closely related narrative that presents a rather darker picture. Here nostalgia for a lost wholeness produces a resistance to disciplinary structures. The rise of the disciplines is interpreted as a divisive process which resulted in the administrative confinement of the subversive intellect (or human spirit) and is explicitly named as an exercise in order and control. Behind this perspective stands the work of Kant ([1798] 1979) and those Enlightenment philosophers who advocated resistance to the fragmentation of knowledge. In the political ferment of the 1960s, this interpretation of disciplinarity was taken up and modified within a variety of emancipatory movements that not only viewed the maintenance of academic disciplines as the consequence of a bureaucratization of knowledge but also saw the disciplines as actively engaged in marginalizing the concerns and the wisdom of non-dominant groups. It was the disciplines which enabled cultural silence to be maintained on some of the most pressing political questions of our time. A new 'critical interdisciplinarity' was taking shape which invited researchers not to become settlers in virgin territory ('vacant interdisciplinarity') but to dispute the colonization of knowledge by disciplinary powers. From the perspective of his interdisciplinary work in Canadian Studies Arthur Kroker offers a useful summary of the salient features of critical interdisciplinarity. These are identified as: collective thinking on shared problems of pressing concern neglected by mainstream scholarship; a re-evaluation of memories and narratives not previously deemed significant; the strategic invention of discourses able to represent new identities adequately; a form of knowledge creation that is public, located, transformative and accountable (Kroker, 1980). Commitment to interdisciplinarity as a form of critical praxis remains a motivating force for many researchers who have chosen the insecure location of interdisciplinary study instead of making their homes within more established academic structures.

The language of critique draws me to the third narrative of interdisciplinarity, one which is particularly significant within literature and theology.

Poststructuralist theory has offered a compelling analysis of the regulative nature of disciplinary power which is frequently rehearsed by those who stress the liberating potential of interdisciplinary research. Foucault's work (for example 1994; 2002) is the most widely quoted and well known. His archaeological investigations chart the configuration of knowledge and power in the development of the disciplines and other poststructuralist theorists have added their own contribution to this critique (see Soussioff and Franco 2002). Important though these interventions have been, it is not primarily the critique of the disciplines that has been poststructuralism's major contribution to current forms of interdisciplinarity, but rather the provision of a metatheoretical language that is spoken across many disciplines and its configuration of theoretical analysis as a work of intricate reading; interpreting culture through its 'texts' and what is written 'on the body'. In his tirade against the conventions of contemporary academia, *After Theory* (2004), Terry Eagleton describes this theoretical hegemony as a tidal wave rolling 'across linguistics, philosophy, literature, politics, art, anthropology and so on, breaching academic barriers as it went. It was a library cataloguer's nightmare' (2004: 69).

And not only disturbing for librarians! For Eagleton too this deluge is deeply problematic. He is concerned at the lack of political responsibility that appears in the wake of 'high theory'. Although the turn to language and culture has resulted in a renewed interest in the politics of everyday life, it has deflected attention away from issues of larger concern. 'On the wilder shores of academia,' he complains, 'an interest in French philosophy has given way to a fascination with French kissing ... the politics of masturbation exert more fascination than the politics of the Middle East ... the body is an immensely fashionable subject but it is the erotic body not the famished body' (Eagleton 2004: 2). He is disturbed by the image of postgraduate students liberated from the constraint of their 'faculties' writing their PhDs on issues previously deemed unsuitable for academic study but lacking the resources to subject these to serious critique (2004: 3).

It would be true to say that many feminists stand in a similarly ambivalent relation to poststructuralism, which challenges macro analyses of patriarchal power, the notion of women's experience and even the category 'woman' itself. In contrast, numerous others have found that a discourse founded upon alterity, difference, and, more lately, hybridity and queer couplings, can be as politically productive as one predicated upon equality, essence and identity. As Judith Butler has argued, 'The deconstruction of identity is not the deconstruction of politics ... If identities were no longer fixed as the premises of a political syllogism, a new politics would surely emerge from the ruins of the old' (1990: 148).

No such political anxieties assail some of the more radical exponents of poststructuralism, of whom there are a number working in literature and theology. They would understand it as a profoundly destabilizing movement, the discursive herald of a new age and the harbinger of a fundamental shift in our epistemic system (that is to say also our culture, way of life and being in the world). In this frame the multiple, mystical, tongues with which it speaks can not be disassociated from the murmurings which reach from the holocausts of the previous century, the travail of our global ecology and a world where the collapse of foundationalism contests with the rise of fundamentalism. In this frame the tremors felt within the disciplines are evidence of an underground explosion with far greater destructive power than has yet been realized.

'Crossing (out) the disciplines'?[2]

I have described three 'narratives' of interdisciplinarity which coexist in the contemporary academy and which are all evident within contemporary work on literature and theology. The first form of interdisciplinarity represents a sensible pooling of resources, a borrowing and sharing between disciplines, an ethical commitment to work together for the common good and the advancement of knowledge. All that is best in the disciplines is cherished and preserved but new and creative leaps forward become possible. The second has a much more critical approach to the construction of knowledge. Seeing disciplinary boundaries as maintained for purposes of order and control, it regards interdisciplinarity as a form of academic praxis that is most suited to transforming social structures. The third form of interdisciplinarity represents a common theoretical discourse spoken across the faculties. This does not so much contend with the disciplines as deconstruct their authority, shifting the familiar terrain and assaulting the foundations of knowledge.

Up to this point I have made few specific mentions of feminist perspectives on interdisciplinary study. Women have embraced interdisciplinarity for all of the practical, critical and deconstructive reasons outlined above and the existence of 'Women's Studies' within many university contexts represents one of the most sustained projects in interdisciplinary cooperation to have emerged within the contemporary academy. The terms 'undisciplined' or 'wild' have been used to signal the rejection of the traditional ways of categorizing knowledge within Women's Studies (see, for example, Buker, 2003) and for some feminist researchers interdisciplinarity remains the only feasible way to produce authentic and, more importantly, transformative accounts of women's experience. Renate Klein, for example, argues that:

---

[2]   A resonant phrase coined by Ruth Salvaggio in a paper presented at the Modern Language Association annual meeting in 1992. See Pryse 1998 for a discussion of the term.

Since the drama of 'life' does not take place in a glass womb ... subject compartmentalisation must be broken down in order to both study and survive ... the compartmentalisation of knowledge was – and by some of us still is – explicitly opposed. (R. Klein, in Allen and Kitch 1998: 275)

The commitment to interdisciplinarity has been strengthened through efforts to generate feminist understandings of epistemology. After the work of Sandra Harding (1991), Donna Haraway (1991a) and others on strong objectivity[3] and situated knowledge[4], many feminists came to regard dialogical interactions across a range of perspectives as one of the authenticating marks of valid claims to 'know', 'understand' or 'tell the truth' about *any* situation or issue. It has also been argued that attention to differing perspectives contributes to the formation of hybrid (Haraway 1991b: 148–81), nomadic (Braidotti 1994) or 'meztisa' (Anzaldúa 1993) feminist identities. These subject positions are portrayed as responsive to diversity and postmodern pluralism in ways that do not entail relinquishing the feminist project of social transformation. It is argued that those who have experienced alienation within dominant discourses and whose identity is located at a point of intersection between different traditions are best able to navigate the shift from:

> habitual formations; from convergent thinking, analytical reasoning that tends to use rationality to move towards a single goal (a Western mode), to divergent thinking characterized by movement away from set patterns and goals toward a more whole perspective, one that includes rather than excludes. (Anzaldúa 1993: 429)

However, not all feminists are ready to bid farewell to the disciplines, and some are now arguing for a reappraisal of the value of disciplinary study. Disciplines are shared traditions of enquiry and these have important functions, such as providing a common language, establishing a structure of colleagueship, and critiquing thought. Those who are not located within disciplinary structures often find themselves lacking power and

---

[3]   Strong objectivity requires that a person seeking knowledge attends to those with different concerns and understandings of the issues in question and particularly to the insights of those whose lives are most affected by the concerns under debate. This enables them not only to come to a fuller understanding but also to gain an awareness of how their own knowledge and opinions are related to their context and experience (see Harding 1991: 151).

[4]   Concerning situated knowledge Haraway writes:

> Above all rational knowledge does not pretend to disengagement: to be from everywhere and so nowhere, to be free from interpretation, from being represented, to be fully self-contained or fully formalisable. Rational knowledge is a process of ongoing critical interpretation among fields of interpreters and decoders. Rational knowledge is power sensitive conversation. (1991a: 196)

influence (and money, tenure and status!) within the academy. In a thoughtful essay upon whether women should be encouraged to abandon their disciplinary allegiances Susan Stanford Friedman acknowledges the negative impact interdisciplinarity can have upon the career prospects of women. She also maintains that although disciplines can be understood (after Foucault) as the product of an 'institutional organization of knowledge characterized by a discursive system with regulatory, coercive effects that confine knowledge within certain sets of limiting boundaries' (1998: 313), they can also stimulate rigour and a patient, painstaking form of creativity. She then proceeds to advocate a reappraisal of disciplinarity:

> I prefer a locational approach that acknowledges the potentially positive as well as negative effects of knowledge boundaries, The word's resonance with systematic, sustained and highly skilled labour, even craftsmanship, is as significant for me as its association with punishment. (1998: 313)

Friedman's approach is a helpful one which recalls that interdisciplinarity, even emancipatory or critical interdisciplinarity, need not necessarily imply the abolition of subject-specific traditions of enquiry. There are now feminists working to critique most disciplines from the perspective of committed insiders, often borrowing the tools they need to do so from outside their designated field of scholarship. Whilst some still argue that the existence of feminist anthropology, philosophy or economics (for example) strengthens rather than subverts the male-centred hegemony of the disciplines, most would recognize the real value of employing a deep awareness of disciplinary conventions when subjecting these to challenge or envisaging their reconstruction.

A perspective that recognizes boundaries but is prepared to cross them does not, therefore, necessarily imply the desire to overthrow the faculties. Indeed it presents great scope for initiatives of strategic transgression. This is an especially significant point when we are talking about disciplines that are not traditionally regarded as cognate, but sometimes seen as oppositional. This is the case with literature and theology, which may be taken as representative of conflicting ways of apprehending the world (see page 35). The value of interdisciplinary study in such cases may not be the sharing, and is certainly not the merging, of knowledge; it is more a point of exploring the tensions between powerful discourses. As I argue later (see pp. 37–8), if feminists simply ignore the conventions of disciplinarity they are unable to make a distinctive contribution to important debates that are taking place at those interesting places where disciplines clash and contradict. This is to relinquish voluntarily some very fertile fields of academic research which then become the exclusive possession of the sons and heirs.

Literature and theology

After this long detour necessary to place discussions of literature and theology in context I now return to the specific concern of this chapter: the interdisciplinary study of literature and theology. My way into analysing contemporary trends in this area has been to employ as a vantage point my experience as an editor of the journal *Literature and Theology*. I chose the journal as my focus both because I can employ my insider knowledge to interpret what I find, and also because the journal holds a special and privileged place in this area of study.

Founded some twenty years ago with the aim of fostering research 'of serious interest to both theologians and students of literature',[5] the journal was born at a significant moment. The first editors declared, '*Literature and Theology* marks the beginning of a new phase in the development of an increasingly significant interdisciplinary area' (Jasper *et al* 1987: iii). The editors believed that literary critics were at last beginning to pay serious attention to religious themes, and common concerns with narrative, hermeneutics, myth and canonicity were becoming apparent between the disciplines. The first editor, David Jasper, noted the emergence of new directions in critical theory and offered a cautious welcome to those elements of 'value in the deconstructive exercise' (1987: 9).

Although joining together in heralding a new epoch, most of the founding editors of the journal were firmly located within traditional areas of study such as Victorian literature or romanticism and the journal has continued to walk a difficult path between a deep respect for the rigours of disciplinarity and radical new thinking. Indeed it has been necessary on a number of occasions to signal that radical and critical perspectives are particularly welcome. There has never been a shortage of contributions on topics such as 'Poetry in the Book of Common Prayer' or 'God in Milton', but it has often proved harder to attract articles pushing interdisciplinary boundaries in radical or experimental ways.

Today *Literature and Theology* is established as a prestigious and successful publication with an international readership and is widely regarded as a leading publication in the field. It has strong links with the International Society for Religion, Literature and Culture and regularly publishes the material from their biennial conferences. Although it has the look and feel of a traditional scholarly journal (a fact that its publishers, Oxford University Press, regard as a positive economic asset!) it has not abandoned its radical editorial policy and can be distinguished from other journals in the field by its non-confessional stance and its enthusi-

---

[5]   From the statement of intent published on the inside cover of the journal in its early years. This statement has been revised on numerous occasions and these revisions are themselves of interest to the researcher.

astic embrace of contemporary theory. So what can an analysis of material published in the journal uncover of the concealed history of interdisciplinarity? In particular, what can this method show about the significance of gender in literature and theology?

Counting heads

In order to address these questions, I analysed articles published over a six-year period.[6] The majority, 62 per cent, were written solely by men. It might be thought that the fact that the remaining 38 per cent were written or co-authored by women does not represent a disgraceful gender balance within a prestigious academic journal – the more highly regarded the vehicle, the less likely women are to secure a ride. However, my insider's knowledge allows me to disclose that a good number of the articles written by women were commissioned[7] and, furthermore, that the editorial team made other special efforts to generate contributions from women.[8] This is not to imply that women's published writing was of a lower quality; it was subjected to the same rigorous refereeing system as men's work. Rather, submissions from women were rarer than is apparent and had to be sought out.

Disappointing as the picture of men actively seeking publication and women being enticed into this field might be, it is not particularly shocking. What I did find a much more startling result of my research was the fact that many articles contained no reference to women at all. In over 90 per cent of men's articles the only reference to women was as incidental characters in books, plays or films or in minor academic supporting roles (such as footnote references). *None* of these articles focused on the work of significant women authors or theorists. Of the remaining articles written by men in which women did appear, the majority were on the canonized female authors (such as Austen, Eliot and Woolf). There was one article critiquing male power and two contained significant references to the work of both genders.

This deeply depressing picture is replicated when women's articles are analysed. Nearly half of these (42 per cent) were solely concerned with the work of male artists/writers or theorists, while a further 10 per cent

---

[6]   A total of 171 articles published between 1997 and 2003.

[7]   The journal editor for the bulk of the period under consideration was Graham Ward. He is one of the few male theologians working in Britain today to have engaged deeply with feminist poststructuralist theory and who includes insights from this study in his published works. He drew significantly on this knowledge, and his networks in this field, to encourage contributions from women during his time as editor.

[8]   For example, in 2001 the journal sponsored a conference, 'Deeply Material', on spiritual themes in women's writing to stimulate new work in this field.

contained references to works by men and women. In all, nearly three-quarters of published articles were exclusively concerned with the work of men. *It must be remembered that many of the remaining contributions which do refer to women were specifically sought out or generated by the editors of the journal.*

A head count such as this presents an immediate picture of how much an interdisciplinary area such as literature and theology can replicate the continuing predominance of male-centred scholarship within the academy; interdisciplinarity, in itself, does not challenge this hegemony. It demonstrates where power and influence are located but is otherwise a rather crude instrument of analysis. I now turn to a closer reading of the texts themselves.

Close reading

In the founding statement of the journal[9] the editors identified some of the common themes that were emerging in the study of literature and theology and encouraged contributors to address these in a manner fruitful to both disciplines. Despite this open invitation to explore semiotics, hermeneutics, myth and methodology, throughout the journal's history it has been articles focusing on religious themes in art and literature which have predominated.[10] Usually these articles focus upon a specific text or artwork. Taken together, these account for 73 per cent of the articles written by men and 85 per cent of the articles written by women.

In what way can this form of writing be seen as interdisciplinary? Clearly, in terms of the first model discussed it represents a 'borrowing and sharing' across disciplinary boundaries. For example, better scholarship on George Eliot's *Daniel Deronda* is produced when we take account of her evangelical period and her encounter with the work of Strauss and Feuerbach. Similarly, an awareness of narrative theory has played a huge role in contemporary readings of the Gospel of Mark. Bringing together the two disciplines in order that one can shed light upon concerns within the other is important and useful. Work of this kind is

---

[9]   The first editorial statement, appearing on the inside front cover of the journal, states:

> Both theology and literature have given serious attention to a number of mutual issues using different and sometimes contradictory critical tools. Of mutual interest, for example, are narrative, the historical content of literature, the nature of myth, the study of language and semiotics, the art of translation and hermeneutics … The journal welcomes analysis of individual texts so long as they raise general questions relevant to both disciplines.

[10]   With these I have included literary readings of sacred texts.

consistently generated by those theologians who love literature and literary critics who acknowledge the importance of religion. It is self-evidently an academically worthy exercise and this probably accounts for the fact that the interdisciplinary terrain of 'literature and theology' is not viewed as a wild and undisciplined region but has attained its own niche within the academy.

It is not possible to draw a firm line between articles that simply 'share and borrow' and those that use interdisciplinarity to reshape dominant conventions – the effects of sharing and borrowing may be more trans-formative than expected. However, my readings suggest that the bulk of the articles on religious themes in art and literature have no such intent or outcome. Occasionally, however, articles of this kind do veer towards 'critical interdisciplinarity' when they recover forgotten voices, make explicit radical insights that have been previously neglected, or draw upon resources in one discipline to *critique* the other. There are a number of such articles in the period under analysis and, perhaps unsurprisingly, the majority of these are written by women. Those articles on religious themes in art and literature that have an explicit feminist perspective frequently employ interdisciplinarity in order to shift received interpre-tations of a text or reclaim neglected works that are significant for women. Although the sample base is too small to make significant claims, it does also appear that women may be more willing to risk 'deep inter-disciplinarity' than men. Fascinating work links Le Corbusier, Rabelais and St Teresa, or Augustine and Mary Daly, for example. Men appear to be less eclectic and tend to begin from a secure base in one location and reach out towards another.

If there are relatively few articles in my sample that could be straight-forwardly classed as being in the tradition of critical interdisciplinarity, there are a significant number which adopt the third mode of interdis-ciplinarity explored above. Theory-based articles which resist disciplinary categorization accounted for 27 per cent of male contributions and the philosophers of choice in the period under examination were Derrida (the most popular), Levinas, Benjamin, Nietzsche and Heidegger. Most articles with a theoretical focus written by men employed the theorist to make some form of cultural analysis and a number of these had radical social or ethical subtexts – although these were seldom foregrounded in the discussion. Women contributed fewer theory-based articles, accounting for only 15 per cent of their contributions. The work of women philoso-phers was presented within these works and Butler, Kristeva and Irigaray were the most popular. When writing on theory, women often played the role of advocate or instructor, introducing significant elements of the work of a woman thinker (who may be assumed to be unfamiliar to the reader) rather than applying theory in a work of cultural interpretation.

From this analysis of the interdisciplinary terrain a more detailed picture begins to emerge. If *Literature and Theology* is used as an indicator, then it appears that the field is a segregated one in which male-centred scholarship prevails. As well as constituting a minority group, when women do contribute articles, in almost half of cases their work is indistinguishable from that of male colleagues. They write about the same male authors, the same male theorists and the same male-centred critical controversies. Women contribute significantly fewer articles on theory than their male counterparts and are more tentative in applying theory to cultural texts. Despite a greater willingness shown by women to consider female authors and theorists, it would be an error to assume that articles written by women will display feminist commitments. We are certainly not witnessing within *Literature and Theology* a determined feminist-inspired intervention to destabilize and democratize this academic border zone. All of which leaves me with two questions to consider:

1. Why is feminist writing on literature and theology not having a greater impact upon academic interdisciplinary debate?
2. Why do men working in this field not engage with women's critical and creative work?

I will address each of these briefly in conclusion to this chapter but my hope is that my rather fragmentary responses will provoke further research into the concealed reality of interdisciplinarity in the future.

The good girls and the clever boys

In the previous chapter I made clear how important literature has been for religious feminists and argued that it had made a huge impact upon feminist theology, the significance of which we are only now beginning to realize. Why are the women who so confidently write about Lessing, Walker, Morrison and others in monographs and feminist journals not contributing to other debates in the academy on literature and theology? Why is their work not influencing the scholarly agenda? Even the most cursory reading of the work of women like Christ, Ostriker, Sands and Brock would offer some clues. Their style, language, implied audience, authorial voice and issues of concern are markedly different from those addressed in forums such as *Literature and Theology*.

When I mentioned the results of my research to a male colleague who has contributed to the journal he remarked, somewhat shamefacedly as women had not attained footnote status in his own article, 'I would have included women but no girls have written anything clever enough for *Literature and Theology*.' This humorous comment has an element of truth within it. Despite the radical sympathies of many of the editorial team, the pages of *Literature and Theology* constitute an elite space for 'clever' conversations. To be sure the journal welcomes contributions by women but those published tend to be written in a familiar language that reassures the reader of either their disciplinary competence or theoretical sophistication. We must ask whether the elite tone of the journal works to produce subtle forms of self-censorship and is in itself therefore inherently conservative?

That feminist discourse is unfamiliar does not, of course, imply that it is naïve or insubstantial. However, to those unfamiliar with its distinct epistemology, hermeneutics and critical categories it can appear to be so. Toril Moi has further argued that, in the current academic climate, referring to feminists' concerns at all can sound anachronistic, unfashionable and unsophisticated. It may be acceptable for women who are self-identified feminist academics (and enjoy the security of academic tenure or a niche status in the publishing world) to continue to do so but it is not likely to offer a pathway to success for the ambitious male – or younger woman either. The result is that:

> Women find themselves as marginalized as they ever were in theory-related contexts. I mean more marginalized than in 1985. Lots of big theoretical debates carry on – about meaning and modernity and so on – and people make their contributions, write, give lectures and write their papers, and they'll be very theoretically sophisticated but there won't be a word about women or feminism in them ... Back in 1985 the whole point of having feminist theory was that concerns that had to do with women were supposed to be as important as all other concerns in every theoretical context ... Well no longer so apparently. It annoys me also that it's only women who keep on mentioning this sorry state of affairs. Just as I can discuss modernity with him, a male theorist ... could discuss women's and feminism's place in modernity with me, right? Well, it's just not happening. (2003: 135)

Toril Moi makes the important point here that even when women are theoretically literate, once they wish to employ theory to address issues of concern to women then there is an immediate sense that the tone of debate has been lowered and something less important/less interesting is now taking place. This impacts upon the way the theoretical work of religious feminists is read within the academy. But we must also note that many religious feminists seek to write in straightforward, accessible tones and actively resist theoretical discourse, believing it to be male centred, obscure, alienating and dangerous. For these women, poststructuralism represents a turning away from what Linda Curti calls 'the political real' (1998: 1) and undermines the ethical and emancipatory ideals that are the defining marks of feminist theology.

Within a generally sceptical approach to theory there is a further marked reluctance on the part of this body of religious feminists to use poststructuralist theory in relation to women's literature. Less aversion exists in employing deconstructive techniques to critique the 'male' canon and tradition! However, a strong sense of the sacredness of women's writing still prevails. This is bound up with an attachment to the idea of the woman author who is frequently portrayed as conveying a *gendered identity* to her texts. As women's literary texts are often ranged against the 'male' texts of the theological tradition it is strategically very important to maintain this connection. '[I]t is the author who guarantees the presence of this difference by her womanhood', argues Chris Weedon (1987: 154).[11] It is interesting that those articles published in *Literature and Theology* that do offer overtly feminist readings of literary and artistic texts are not relying upon poststructuralist theory to any great extent. They are more likely to employ the tools developed within gynocriticism over twenty years ago.[12] Reclaiming, remembering and revisioning are still the most popular approaches, and although the content of the articles might be radical, the reading strategies themselves are largely still conventional.

If the third form of interdisciplinarity, based on a shared metatheoretical language, is not attractive to many religious feminists engaging with literature, what about the first model based upon a pragmatic sharing across disciplinary boundaries? This is also problematic, but for different reasons. The majority of feminist theologians who use women's literature in their reflections on the divine do not tend to see it as literature (it is frequently referred to by the intergeneric term 'women's writing'). It functions as the only textual source available for feminist scholarship before the modern era and must suffice in place of theology – and philosophy, history, sociology and political theory etc. Contemporary women's writing is similarly put to a variety of uses without critical appraisal. This indiscriminate use of literature has led to the charge that feminist theologians have not yet learned to read! They deny the

> *fictional* as well as the *literary* character of the text: life and literature overflow into each other ... The difference between persons and characters fades. Literature appears to be a realistic reflection of experiences: the notion that literature is a constructed representation appears to be absent.[13]
> (van Heijst 1995: 261)

---

[11] Weedon further writes:

> The concept of authorship which guarantees most feminist readings of black, white and lesbian women's writing is shared with liberal-humanist criticism. The author is the speaking, full, self-present subject producing the text from her own knowledge of the world and she is the guarantee of its truth. (Weedon 1987: 162)

[12] Most of the techniques used within feminist articles in literature and theology are to be found in Elaine Showalter's pioneering edited collection *The New Feminist Criticism: Essays on Women, Literature and Theory* (1986a).

[13] Van Heijst's criticism was made of Carol Christ but the same critique could be applied to other religious feminists.

Not only is literature 'un-disciplined' in this process, but religious feminists often do not regard their own work as theology either. The notion of inter-disciplinarity as a sharing of previously restricted disciplinary resources is meaningless for these women.[14] Of the three models of interdisciplin-arity introduced in the first pages of this chapter the most appealing to religious feminists, namely critical interdisciplinarity, is the least prominent in the pages of the journal – and, indeed, beyond those pages at the present time.

The silence of the straights

I had expected to find that women contributors and women's concerns were under-represented in the pages of *Literature and Theology*. I was not surprised by the fact that many women chose to focus on the work of men. What did shock me was the almost total lack of interest male contributors showed in the significant work produced by women writers, philosophers and theologians in recent times. Germaine Greer once commented, 'Women have very little idea of how much men hate them' (1993 [1971]: 279). I do not know if men hate women but I have discovered most appear profoundly disinterested in their creative work. It is interesting to speculate on the reasons why this might be so.

In a recent article, Bjorn Krondorfer (2007) explores the lack of interest heterosexuals (particularly men)[15] show in gay theology. This interdiscip-linary area brings together gender studies, queer theory and theology and is the site of lively scholarship and debate. Like me, Krondorfer explored the mainstream of peer-reviewed journals and found an 'almost complete silence' regarding significant works of gay scholarship even in the work

---

[14]   Similarly, there are feminist literary critics addressing the use of the sublime in modern women's literature but they are not applying theological categories to interpret what they find. This may be because the spirituality they encounter in women's artistic work is often heterodox, mystical or employs female representations of the divine: theology is not at its most useful in relation to any of these categories. However, I think it is also the case that many feminist literary critics are simply unaware of the theological traditions that have shaped some significant literary work by women. Some very useful 'borrowing and sharing' might take place if literary critics working on the female sublime could overcome their aversion to theology and familiarize themselves with key concepts and themes. I have in mind particularly here the literary work of women writing in the middle of the last century whose work often contains very sophisticated engagement with religious thinking of their time and who prefigure many of the ideas later taken up within feminist theology (for example: H. D., Elizabeth Smart, P. L. Travers, Etty Hillesum). There is much more widely available and excellent scholarship on the religious thinking and piety of women writers from the nineteenth century and up to the First World War.
[15]   There is a greater openness to the insights of lesbians within feminist theology although this has been, and continues to be, an area of tension. The fact that so many women theologians are lesbians must be an important factor here.

of authors who 'are not from the homophobic religious right but represent the liberal-minded world that is generally supportive of gay men' (2007). This silence, he argues, speaks very loudly, but how do we interpret it? Krondorfer offers five possible reasons for this colossal non-response.

The first is *indifference*, which he links to an anxiety concerning professional reputation as discussed above. The second is *radical transgression of disciplinary boundaries* in the work of gay theologians. This represents a move beyond what is commonly perceived to be interdisciplinarity and, Krondorfer argues, frequently results in academic marginalization. My analysis above would suggest that feminist theologians may have similarly violated disciplinary conventions to such an extent that their work on literature and theology no longer fits traditional notions of interdisciplinarity. They have placed themselves beyond the pale. The third reason, the *gaying of religion*, Krondorfer maintains, is threatening to male scholars as alternative histories, hagiographies and religious meanings invade their cloistered spaces, triggering anxieties concerning institutional purity, authority and the sexualization of a spiritual domain. A 'gay appropriation of the sacred is prone to hostile reactions' (2007: 266), Krondorfer argues, and I would argue that so is a feminine one. The topics that male interdisciplinary scholarship in literature and theology has loved to debate (existential angst, the quest for meaning and identity, absurdity and nihilism, the struggle with/against God – all those bleak and beautiful eternal questions) are not illuminated by the parochial and personal concerns of women. Lastly, gay theologians' *autobiographical insertions and erotic confessions*, which render both author and reader vulnerable, are not only in defiance of academic conventions but, Krondorfer believes, generate in straight men an uneasy and unpleasant 'squeamishness', which might be classically identified as a repugnance at the return of the repressed. My own observation of the way my male students and colleagues struggle with the bodily texts of women would support this observation!

All these factors conspire to create a situation, Krondorfer argues, in which the fear of contamination and pollution is such that engaging with such alien discourse represents an unacceptable risk for straight men. My perception is that male scholars sense that embracing the work of women might produce similarly 'polluting' effects. Their tones are disappointingly vulgar, they are transgressive, they domesticate and feminize the sacred spaces, their texts can be 'icky' and uncomfortable and too tied to ambivalent desires. Best left alone. And luckily, men have a perfect excuse to do so. Having learned rather painfully in the 1980s and 90s not to speak on behalf of women, they have now discovered, in the changed atmosphere of a postfeminist millennium, it is more profitable not to speak about them at all.

Chapter 3

Literature and Theology: Sex in the Relationship

The dream of harmony

My research interests lie in the cross-disciplinary study of literature and theology and particularly in bringing feminist insights to bear upon the way in which the relationship between these disciplines is constructed in academic debate. It might be supposed that this would entail a meticulous attention to the definition of terms – 'What is theology?', 'What is literature?' However, whilst this work is undeniably important it quickly becomes apparent that the disciplinary boundaries are hard to define; it is almost impossible to make a definitive separation between literary and theological genres and political considerations are often paramount in deciding where a line is to be drawn.

This indeterminacy might be thought to raise serious problems for the researcher. However, any reader of the extensive writing on literature and theology will soon become aware that whatever disciplinary definitions are being offered these are of secondary importance to what is implied by the supposed difference between the two categories. There is clearly some relation between actual, what might be termed 'shelveable', texts of literature and theology and what is meant when the words theology or literature are employed in debate. The terms are burdened with the associations they carry and are used *heuristically* to convey contrasting approaches to issues of fundamental concern. In this sense current inter-disciplinary debates have an extended genealogy going back at least as far as discussions between philosophy and poetry in the work of Plato and Aristotle (see Cupitt 1991: 40).

The term 'theology' trails in its wake notions of a negotiable and intelligible universe. Because the purposes of God are communicable through revelation, and because human beings are endowed with a rationality that mirrors that of their creator, it is possible to strive towards clarity, universality and reasonable certainty when we give expression to faith. In order to achieve clarity a process of abstraction and a purification of forms is necessary and desirable. While there will always remain a mystery at the heart of things, theology strives towards the light. It seeks to generate the illumination necessary to live by faith in this world.

In contrast literature is frequently employed to evoke what is contrary, particular and resists abstraction or incorporation into systematic thought. In parable, metaphor and allegory it confounds interpretation. Straying from the straight and narrow, literature is profligate in the production of new meanings. Literature overwhelms plain sense with beauty and gives voice to pain that cannot be carried in other forms. It is reckless in its approach to the established conventions of everyday life.

It becomes apparent that literature and theology are thus commonly located on opposite sides of a binary schema through which meaning is generated in Western culture. Theology is placed on the side of spirit, reason, light, truth, order, God. Literature is associated with the body, desire, darkness, mystery, humanity. Theology is the place where God and 'man' meet. Literature, like Lilith excluded from the garden, endlessly seduces and gives birth. This binary and hierarchical division has been the unstated assumption behind classical formulations of the relations between the disciplines.

The poet T. S. Eliot is the most widely quoted representative of what might be termed a conservative understanding of the relationship between literature and theology. Eliot was convinced of the importance of both religion and art to a healthy culture. However, he held that the religious faith of a people sustains and enlivens the whole. Christians should strive for an organic society in which there is a healthy functioning 'social-religious-artistic complex' (Eliot 1951: 62). But they should never lose sight of the fact that it is theology that should guide literary judgements.

Literature is thus viewed as having an important role to play but requiring the guiding hand of theology to regulate its energy and potentially harmful influence. Eliot is particularly concerned to warn against the dangers that ensue when literature abandons its appointed place and seeks to usurp the authority of theology. He opposed those 'who would make literature a substitute for a definitive theology or philosophy' and dedicated himself to 'try to keep the old distinction clear' (in Kojecky 1971: 76). Quoting Jacques Maritain, a thinker he deeply admired, he proclaimed that literature needs theology to save it from itself. 'By showing where moral truth and the genuine supernatural are situated religion saves poetry from the absurdity of believing itself destined to transform ethics and life: saves it from overweening arrogance' (Maritain, in Lucy 1960: 134).

In Eliot's thought it is clear that theology performs the duties of the good husband and literature represents the wife. If proper relations between the couple are maintained then harmony prevails. Literature in her own sphere is worthy of honour but unrestrained she has the power to damage the common cultural home.[1] Whilst Eliot's work represents perhaps the most clearly articulated understanding of a hierarchy between literature and theology, the idea of a complementary and harmonious relation is one which continues to be widely held.

In contrast to this conservative position Terence Wright is keen to honour both disciplines and his work presents a scholarly and creative exposition of the challenges and insights that literature offers to theology. He writes:

> There will always be a tension between conceptual and creative discourse. Systematic theology will continue the necessary attempt to impose clarity and consistency upon language while literature will no doubt maintain its equally necessary task to complicate and enrich the apparent security of theological concepts. (1988: 13)

Paul Fiddes pictures a similar harmonious division between the literary and theological imaginations. The impulse of theology is to make manifest God's self-disclosure. In a contrary manner literature reminds humanity of a reality reason cannot comprehend:

> Christian theologians, appealing to revelation, and writers employing imagination understand themselves as working in two rather different directions. The first are following a movement from mystery towards image and story, the second, from image and story *towards* a mystery. (Fiddes 1991: 27)

Theology seizes language to illuminate and instruct whereas literature leads us back towards the dark and damp, sacred places where words and forms disintegrate.

Although she writes about philosophy rather than theology, the work of Martha Nussbaum is important to consider here. She presents perhaps the most sustained contemporary reflection on the complementary

---

[1] T. S. Eliot's views on the proper relations between literature and theology have their counterpart in his views concerning the proper relations between women and men. Commenting upon the Nazi determination to locate the energies of women in the kitchen, childcare and church he argued that this idea could not be dismissed simply because of its fascist origins. 'Might one suggest that the kitchen, children and church could be considered to have a claim upon the attention of married women? Or that no normal married woman would prefer to be a wage earner if she could help it?' (1939: 69–70)

relations between rational, abstract forms of discourse and creative writing. Her work has been extremely influential in both feminist and theological debate.[2] Crucial to Nussbaum's argument is the acknowledgement that there may be some views of the world and how one should live in it, especially those that emphasize its complexity and mysteriousness, that cannot be fully and adequately stated in the language of conventional philosophical prose. Nussbaum advocates an opening up of philosophy to receive the insights of literature. Literary texts are invaluable resources for the philosopher because they testify to the mystery and beauty of human life and what is more they carry emotion into the world of practical reason.

On an initial reading it might appear that Nussbaum is a defender of literature and adamant in her insistence that 'literature cannot be reduced to philosophical example' (1986: 14). However, a critical reading of her work reveals that literature is seen as a necessary supplement to philosophy rather than an equal partner. She is selective in the forms of literature she employs and prefers classic texts portraying the great dilemmas of the human condition. She shows less interest in innovatory use of form and does not enquire deeply into whether fiction achieves other ends than reflecting with greater clarity the concerns philosophy has always debated.[3]

In a devastating critique of Nussbaum's project Robert Eaglestone argues that she reinscribes traditional conventions through which the relations between logocentric discourse and literature have always been debated. He concludes that Nussbaum reinstates 'binary oppositions, which can no longer have any value for argument when one side is subsumed in the other' (1997: 58).

If literature is a girl

I have employed the work of Eliot, Wright, Fiddes and Nussbaum to argue that in discussions of the relationship between literature and the

---

[2]   To some feminists her use of literature appears to offer the means of transforming intellectual traditions in a manner that would render them more responsive to material realities of everyday life. Her work has also been used by theologians eager to recover the significance of 'virtue ethics' for Christian practice. Out of her reflections Nussbaum constructs a distinctive Aristotelian discourse on the cultivation of the virtues and the significance of tradition. Nussbaum's work has been widely referenced by theologians. Hauerwas and Jones (1997) include one of her essays in their influential edited collection of work in narrative theology.

[3]   The emotions that literature supposedly embodies are ones that are harnessed to facilitate more effective intellectual enquiry. But literature is not merely a worthy companion for abstract thinking; she is also good in bed. Novels seduce with 'mysterious and romantic charms, they lure into 'a more shadowy and passionate world'. They require the reader 'to assent, to succumb'. (1990: 258)

'logocentric' discourses of theology and philosophy, literature is constructed as female; *literature is a girl*. However, the gendering of literature as female can be understood in a variety of ways. For Eliot it implies that theology has a magisterial role and literature can best serve her purposes through submission to a higher authority. Wright, Fiddes and Nussbaum claim that the 'creative differences' between literature and theology make possible an enriching partnership.

Feminists negotiating these discussions may find themselves irritated by the heterosexual matrix in which this debate is framed and unwilling to enter a discussion predicated on these terms. However, once an awareness of the gendered significance accorded to the terms 'theology' and 'literature' has been achieved it does have critical potential. We can use this understanding to look with fresh eyes at the current theological landscape. Applying the insights of deconstruction we will identify the ways in which the binary schema through which meaning is generated can become disclosive of the ways in which power functions within theological thinking. We will also note how dependent this discourse is upon the elements, which it excludes or denies. Furthermore, we will celebrate the fact that the construction of literature as feminine can no longer signify, as it did for Eliot, a complementary and subservient role.

In the remaining sections of this chapter I shall illustrate the ways in which the heuristic understanding of literature as feminine can be used with deconstructive and disruptive effect to critique two significant trajectories in contemporary theology. I shall then explore how theologians with significant ethical concerns about the nature of theological discourse are employing literature as a means of destabilizing the discipline.

Behind the Bible

In 1974, Hans Frei published *The Eclipse of Biblical Narrative*, a work which was to be of great significance in reconstructing theology as it emerged out of the uncertainty that had besieged it during the previous decade. It is Frei's main argument that through the rise of historical criticism in the eighteenth century the Western churches have lost their sense of the trustworthy and 'realistic' nature of biblical narratives. In articulating this perspective and pleading for a 'return' to biblical narratives Frei draws upon the work of the theologian Karl Barth. Frei's reading of Barth centres upon the notion of God's unique self-revelation in the *story* of Jesus which forms the key to interpreting the rest of scripture and is the foundation of Christian doctrine. Barth argues that in this story we discover our own true story. 'His history as such is our history. It is our own true history (incomparably more direct and intimate than anything we know as our history)' (Barth, in Ford 1981: 165).

As well as Barth, Frei draws upon a classic text of literary theory to construct his understanding of biblical narrative. Erich Auerbach's *Mimesis: The Representation of Reality in Western Literature* (1953) portrays the Bible as a distinctive text in the ancient world. It creates its own universe of meaning which those who encounter it are compelled to enter. 'The Bible's claim to truth is not only far more urgent than Homer's, it is tyrannical – it excludes all other claims. The world of the scripture stories is not satisfied with claiming to be a historically true reality – it claims that it is the only real world' (1953: 14–15). And significantly Auerbach suggests that the Gospel narratives share more in common with the realistic novels of the nineteenth century than they do with other ancient texts (see Loughlin 1996: 76).

By integrating the work of Barth and Auerbach, Frei constructed an alternative to the modern trajectory in biblical studies. Clearly a return to historical literalism was not a credible scholarly option but, he believed, a reawakened sense of the Bible as coherent narrative might restore its use to the churches and generate new grounds for authority in theological thinking.

The project Frei initiated stands in contrast to the attempts of liberal theologians to engage in conversation with contemporary culture. Rather than finding a voice that resonates with common concerns, Christians are to speak in a language that is distinctly their own and distinguishes them from others.[4]

Too much energy has been wasted upon attempts to sustain the illusion that there is compatibility between the Christian faith and the intellectual traditions of the Western world. What is now required is an intercommunal or intratextual effort to generate identity out of the resources of the foundational narratives themselves:

> The most fateful issue for Christian self-description is that of regaining its autonomous vocation as a religion after its defeat in its secondary vocation of providing ideological coherence, foundation and stability to Western culture ... one never knows what this community might then contribute once again to that culture or its residues including its political life, its quest for justice and freedom and even its literature. (1993: 149)

---

[4]   In his later writing Frei draws increasingly upon the work of Lindbeck who likens religious traditions to languages with their own distinctive idioms, symbols and grammatical procedures. It is Lindbeck's conviction that in a situation of 'dechristianization' Christians will be compelled to cultivate their own discursive resources, their 'native tongue', rather than seeking common mediums of cultural exchange (Lindbeck 1984: 33–4).

There are many problems with Frei's project[5] but it is the relation between theology and literature that is of specific concern here. Frei's small aside 'and even its literature' is of immense significance.

Frei is enchanted by literature.[6] As a fervent reader of the great nineteenth-century novels he has learned to approach texts with attention to plot, character, event and action. His Jesus is an agent in a narratable plot (1993: 37). 'The form of the Gospel story is sufficiently novel like' that Jesus may be understood through the same means by which we would understand a character in a realist novel (1993: 46). Frei has learned to surrender himself to the panoramic view of the world presented in the novelistic text and to trust that its 'realism' guarantees the authenticity of all that is there encountered. On all these matters he is quite candid:

> In trying to work out the hermeneutical principles of this program of inter-
> pretation I found that a certain kind of understanding is involved which
> is perhaps best exemplified by what goes on in the 19th century realistic
> novel and in the attempt to understand it … (George Eliot's *Adam Bede*
> and *Middlemarch* come to mind …). (1993: 32)

What enables him to rehearse this position so innocently is the presumption, based on his reading of Auerbach, that it is the Bible which has generated, or pre-empted, this particular literary genre (1993: 46). Indeed, viewed in this light the nineteenth-century novel is not really literature at all. It somehow borrows its 'realism' from the Bible. Frei's critics have poured scorn on the notion that Christians throughout the centuries have employed the conventions appropriate to realistic fiction in their readings of the Bible. What is interesting for the purposes of this text is that a project which is pursued in order to rescue theology from its cultural dependence requires the (invisible) support of literature to sustain it. The concept of biblical narrative employed by Frei is constructed out of the very cultural resources that it is employed to critique. A feminist deconstruction of the canonical narrative theology employed by Frei might begin by exposing the suppressed relation between literature and theology out of which the very notion of 'biblical narrative' is conceived.

The work of Frei, particularly as it has been developed through the encounter with George Lindbeck, has been highly significant to a number of scholars who, from radical or conservative positions, are currently

---

[5]   Most criticisms focus around either the cultural specificity of the reading practice Frei advocates or the problems of engaging in the public sphere on the basis of a self-authenticating narrative.

[6]   I am informed by a colleague that he had a sign on his office door saying 'I'd rather be reading Jane Austen'.

seeking to re-form theology after its long captivity in secular cultural forms. Stanley Hauerwas, for example, understands the Church to be a distinct and peculiar story-formed community. However, in order to describe the dynamics of this countercultural body he is dependent upon literary texts.

His early manifesto *A Community of Character* (1981) is not fabricated around the Gospel stories but around Richard Adams' novel *Watership Down* (1974).[7] In later work it is the novels of Trollope that provide the supplementary material to display the formation of the Christian virtues. He writes:

> I use Trollope because I love to read Trollope. Yet Trollope also helps me display Christian convictions at work … Trollope-like novels are my best allies and resource for the display of the kind of redescriptions required to live as a Christian, particularly in a liberal society. (1994: 8)

Apart from raising intriguing questions about what exactly a 'Trollope-like' novel might be, the extract above prompts questions about the relation between the stories that form communities and 'literature'. As Hauerwas' own work demonstrates, the discreteness of the Christian narrative is illusory. Although narrative might be conceptually distinguished from literature, in reality once narrative is employed as the significant category of analysis it is literary terms and forms that must be used to explicate its function. Once literature is employed we are no longer inhabiting a baptized world of true stories, we are back in the realms of fiction.[8] A feminist hermeneutics of suspicion will allow us to discern in Hauerwas' literary dependence upon the potentially dangerous resources of literature the deconstructive feminine principle which undermines the master narrative.

---

[7]   A novel about a group of rabbits [bucks] seeking to establish a new warren and attract breeding does. I find this choice of text pleasantly ironic.

[8]   As Paul Ricoeur points out, literature may proclaim its faithfulness to reality but this fragile realism is continually undermined by the nature of literary construction:

> If indeed resemblance is only a semblance of truth, what then is fiction under the rule of this semblance but the ability to create the belief that this artifice *stands for* genuine testimony about reality and life? The art of fiction then turns out to be the art of illusion. From here on awareness of the artifice involved undermines from within the realist motivation finally turning against it and destroying it. (1985: 158)

The primal home

In the canonical narrative theologies of Frei and Hauerwas a distinction is being implicitly drawn between realistic narrative[9] and the values of contemporary culture which are seductive, immoral and dangerous.[10] In making this distinction, canonical narrative theologians have used litera-ture to construct theological positions which then erase this vital contri-bution. However, there are alternative understandings of the importance of narrative within theology, which rely upon similarly gendered assump-tions but employ these differently.

In 'The Narrative Quality of Experience' (1997 [1971]), Stephen Crites refuses to disengage narrative from its literary associations and affirms that 'art is involved in all storytelling. It no longer appears natural and innocent in our eyes' (1997: 69). His paper is concerned to establish the culturally generated nature of human identity which is formed through narrative traditions which structure the very nature of experience. We apprehend the world in narrative form.[11]

Crites' understanding of the role of narrative in structuring human experience leads him to the conclusion that the form of narrative is 'primitive' (1997: 82). It engenders human consciousness and communal belonging. It also sustains and protects them. In times of danger, or rapid cultural change, the permeability of narrative forms enables people to perceive new configurations between their experience and the sacred stories of their culture. Literature, as the most significant representative of narrativity, has a crucial role to play in this process of spiritual and social renewal.

The power of Crites' essay lies in the links he proposes between personal biography, sacred traditions and contemporary literary forms. His work has been hugely influential in the development of biographical theology

---

[9]   Established as a genre by the rise of the novel in the modern era and displaying the characteristic concerns of emerging industrial societies.

[10]   However, I have argued that realistic narrative cannot be disassociated from the literary tradition out of which it developed. The realist novel, as Ricoeur has shown, is itself artifice. Milan Kundera goes further and argues that the very style of novelistic realism undermines its own claims to intelligibility and authority. He writes, 'The novel is, by definition, the ironic art. Its "truth" is concealed, undeclared, undeclarable ... It denies our certainties by unmasking the world as an ambiguity' (in Roemer 1995: 145).

[11]   In making this argument Crites distinguishes three forms of narrative. Firstly there are sacred stories which lie 'deep in the consciousness of a people' (1997: 69) forming a mythopoetic inheritance which is anonymous and communal. These stories are 'not like monuments ... but like dwelling places. People live in them' (1997: 69) and they orient the life of a people through time. Secondly there are mundane stories which consist of both the literary resources of culture and the everyday narrative communications that facilitate daily living. 'Here we find stories composed as works of art as well as the much more modest narrative communications that pass between people' (1997: 71). Between sacred and mundane stories there is distinction without separation and mediating between these narrative forms is a third type – that of experience as consciously grasped *always* in narrative form.

and other forms of narrative theology, which emphasize the importance of the cultural construction of identity. As literature is read as a privileged mirror of identity his work paved the way for feminist and black theologians to use literary texts as a theological resource giving voice to those whose reflections on the divine had not been represented in traditional theological discourse (see Goldberg 1991: 12–16).

However, previous discussions have been based upon a hermeneutics of suspicion about the gendered nature of the discourse concerning literature and theology. We can perceive in the work of Crites that what he terms narrative (a territory largely occupied by literature[12]) functions for him as primitive form, maternal home, nurturer and protector – in other words as *good mother*. Clearly this is, in some ways, a more attractive role than wayward wife. However, there are also many problems inherent in this positioning. Literature might easily become associated with a kind of primal goodness that stands in timeless opposition to historical, intellectual and political movements and narrative positioned as primal matter from which all else is formed. These are temptingly attractive notions for Christian thinkers searching for alternative bases for theological thinking after postmodern challenges to foundationalism'.[13] The work of Paul Ricoeur is becoming an increasingly popular resource for narrative constructionists as they seek to establish coherence in a world of chaotic circumstances and fragmented identity. Ricoeur's early writings were constructed in conversational relation to those of Crites (Ricoeur 1991: 141)[14] and like Crites he is concerned with both the cultural and theological import of storytelling, particularly through the literary tradition. Ricoeur presents a process of enplotment as the manner in which human beings 'provide "shape" to what remains chaotic, obscure and mute' (1991: 115). The operation of plotting synthesizes the heterogeneous elements of existence and 'Narration organizes them into an intelligible whole' (1991: 426). This narrative propensity is the basis of our subjectivity/narrative identity as human beings seek to impose the same form of coherence upon the discordances of personal existence.

Whereas canonical narrative theology has not proved a theological position attractive to women,[15] constructive forms of narrative theology

---

[12]   He writes 'narrative is artifice … there have been many forms of narrative epic, drama, history, the novel and so on' (1997: 69).

[13]   See, for example, Peter Hodgson's (2001) recent work on George Eliot.

[14]   Although there are significant differences between the two thinkers, particularly regarding the relation between narrative and symbolism.

[15]   Carol Christ writes that women

> find that self-identification with the sons and other male images and symbols in the language of the Bible and tradition requires us to reject our particular identities as women – the very identities that we are engaged in recovering and affirming in all the other important areas of our lives … the exclusion of our experience from

have been welcomed by religious feminists. For example, Rebecca Chopp (1995: 43) understands 'narrativity' as the primary means through which women are composing their lives in relation to the divine.[16] As such, it is a vital theological activity which now deserves a space in the academy as well as around the kitchen table. In the United States the image of the 'crazy quilt', crafted from worn and irregular pieces of old clothing, frequently stands for the power of women to create form and beauty from obscure and careworn lives.

But feminists are aware that the reclamation of domestic images may prove domesticating. The supposedly natural and primal force of story-telling may be pictured as restoring to women what men have always had: a sense of power of their own agency, the coherence of the social order, the stability of their own identity and an identification with the divine. When viewed in this light, women's storytelling activities may represent nothing more than a form of the constructed foundationalism discussed previously. What if identity is radically plural and fragmented? What if the events of our times are out of joint and cannot be incorporated into a narratable plot? What if God assumes the form of absolute alterity? And what if literature, far from restoring coherence, lends its energies to the unweaving of the world? If these conditions apply, women might be better engaged in pulling the tapestry to pieces rather than forever weaving together the threads. Penelope, I recall, performed both roles.

Reading the disaster

In the previous section I explored the ways in which narrative is currently being used to restore coherence, identity and hope. So significant is narrative's power to remake the world held to be, that the term redemptive has been used to describe its function.

In his book *Telling Stories* Michael Roemer mounts a sustained critique of this position. Roemer maintains that after the last century's genocides 'we no longer believe in character' (1995: 16) and the plot of history has become unintelligible. However, this does not imply for Roemer that storytelling should cease but that the power of storytelling should be reassessed in quite contradictory form.

Roemer argues that an examination of traditional folk narratives reveals that they function not to make the world a safe home but rather to allow humanity to encounter what is strange, unmanageable and *sacred*. In his opinion stories do not in fact order existence. Plot-making

---

the funding of sacred stories may point to a basic defect in the perception of ultimate power and reality provided by the traditional stories. (1979: 230)

[16] Chopp acknowledges a debt to Crites in this understanding (Chopp 1995: 33).

does not signify a fragile mastery of circumstances but enables an encounter with the strange: 'necessity, the sacred, fate, nature, process, time, the past, the generic, and the unconscious – all those things from outside that govern our lives' (1995: 56). In reversing the assumption that narrative conveys order in human affairs Roemer is reinstating his own version of the distinction between literature and theology/philosophy.[17] Fiction may become redemptive precisely because it resists the reconciliation of difference within the subject, in social affairs or between humanity and the sacred:

> Unlike theology it does not comfort us with the presence of an all-knowing, all-powerful deity – who very likely is fashioned from our own needs and who, in turn, often serves for a model of domination and control. Story insists on the utter alterity of the 'other'. (1995: 151)

Roemer's text is a passionate and eclectic critique of attempts to establish narrative coherence in a variety of cultural arenas. However, recently very specific criticisms of narrative as redemptive practice have begun to emerge from amongst the writings of those who are specifically concerned with studying the effects of trauma. In the preface to their edited collection *Tense Past* (1996) Paul Antze and Michael Lambek argue that there is nothing redemptive about subsuming the symbolic/embodied symptoms of trauma into a coherent narrative script. Such scripts are often generated in conventional forms by medical/psychological or social authorities that are seeking not only to heal but also to control those who have experienced trauma.[18] What are circulated as trauma narratives are often attempts by those who have not been subject to such overwhelming circumstances to repair the social fabric by restoring comprehensibility and communication.

Scholars who focus upon the experience of trauma often use the term *testimony* rather than narrative to describe the discourse of trauma survivors themselves. Shoshona Felman writes:

---

[17] He writes:

> Heidegger's conflation of poetry and philosophy and his implied rejection of self-division as an inescapable element in the human condition surely make him susceptible to fascism, which too, claimed a single realm and an actualized wholeness … not only must we pay a steep price for our 'wholeness'; but so must all those whose 'otherness' sustains it. For there *is* no *Volk*, no *Reich*, and very likely no *Führer* without the Jew or his equivalent. (1995:237)

[18] They defy the dominant understanding that to speak one's symptoms is to achieve a release from their disturbing power. 'there is nothing liberating in narrative per se … merely to transfer the story from embodied symptoms to words is not necessarily to exercize it. Development may be foreclosed when a particular version is given complete authority' (Antze and Lambek 1996: xix).

As a relation to events, testimony seems to be composed of bits and pieces of a memory that has been overwhelmed by occurrences that have not settled into understanding or remembrance, acts that cannot be constructed as knowledge nor assimilated into full cognition, events in excess of our frames of reference. (1992a: 5)

By making this distinction Felman is attempting to make a separation between experiences that can be 'told' and those which are incommunicable in realistic terms, but which nevertheless may be given voice through other means. This 'giving of voice' Felman describes as poesis, a translation of experience into strange forms so that inexpressible suffering is 'not given a voice that redeems it from muteness and says it properly but the power to address us in its very silence' (1992b: 163).

In addressing the question 'how can suffering speak?' and suggesting that this may happen through a process of poesis in which metaphor mediates what can never be fully present as narrative, Felman stands in a tradition that has engaged with this problem over the past half-century. The scandal of representing unbearable experience was articulated most powerfully in Theodor Adorno's reflections upon the Holocaust. His initial conclusion was that writing lyrical verses (or indeed engaging in any form of writing) had become impossible after Auschwitz because the world had ceased to be representable in coherent form. He later concluded that the imperative to let suffering speak could only be fulfilled by the metamorphosis of reality which takes place through art and literature (see Felman 1992a: 34).

Adorno's reassessment was made partly on the basis of the literature of testimony which emerged out of the horrors of the Second World War. Paul Celan is a representative figure of those writers who strove to make a mediation of suffering through poetry. Reflecting on this process in a public address given in 1960 [1978] he stated that the poem had become the place in which recognition could be accorded to a silent alterity.

Maurice Blanchot's famous, and fragmented, text *The Writing of the Disaster* articulates similar themes. The disaster is so huge that it is 'the limit of writing' (1995: 7) and de-scribes the world. After such a horror what is it to work at writing? 'To write is to renounce being in command of oneself or having any proper name and at the same time it is not to renounce but to announce, welcoming without recognition the absent' (1995: 121).

What both Celan and Blanchot are reaching towards is an understanding of literature as testimony to what is lost, silent or strange. This, I would argue, is the last way in which we can see the gendering of literature as female in contemporary debate. As Elaine Marks has observed, 'women have always been on the side that has been repressed. Women are the absent, the unacknowledged, the different and the dead' (in Yorke 1991: 113). However, to think only in these terms would be to circumscribe literature as the voice of the powerless victim. Celan is evoking a more active power in poesis, that which makes possible 'the mystery of an encounter' (1978: 37) with the other who confronts and adresses us. This sense of being addressed by the other Carl Raschke has termed the 'epiphany of darkness'. It is this strange epiphany which is the ethical concern of poststructuralist theory. Poststructuralism, as a discourse of alterity, has provided a conceptual vocabulary in which literature is seen as an embodiment in textuality of the 'other' who disrupts the order of the Word. David Pacini explores the effects of this traumatic meeting:[19]

> I am connected to a silence, an ellipsis … Hence I am bound by an obligation of transference, mobilized by the energies of the silenced to become a debtor to the foreign place that static tradition refuses to claim. I am called to the interminable political labour of speaking in the name of the site of the excluded. (1994: 148)

In Pacini's understanding 'being bound by an obligation' is political witness and this theme is further developed by John Caputo in *Against Ethics* (1993). This book develops the notion of obligation as being laid hold of, or claimed, by the other. The other is encountered in the midst of a disaster,[20] and 'Disasters are places where *poems* cluster like leaves trapped in the fissures of windswept walls' (1993: 181, emphasis added). Caputo employs the term 'poetics of obligation'. This 'is a matter of writing other histories, telling other stories, of worrying over other oblivions, of answering other calls' (1993: 166). It involves siding with 'disastrous, disfigured, ill-formed, ill-fated, star-crossed, damaged bodies – with everything that the discourses call flesh' (1993: 194).

Everything the discourses call flesh. That which is bodily, fragile, fertile, desiring, disruptive, female. That which now seizes hold of us and obliges us to respond to its claims. David Jasper argues that literature now confronts theology with the challenge of those things which are 'too often excluded by its systematic claims – laughter, expenditure, meaning-lessness, loss … the scandal and the stumbling block must be reintroduced to overturn the rhetorical machinery of religious power (Jasper 1993: 9).

He argues that instead of settling back into the conservative traditions through which an understanding of the relations between literature and

---

[19]   Pacini's reflections are prompted by the death of his infant son and the effect that had upon his own understanding of faith. The symbolics of poststructuralism give him a voice to express protest, grief and commitment in a radically different form from that of orthodox creedal formulas.

[20]   Caputo refuses the singularity of this term in Blanchot's writing – for him 'life is a disaster' (1993: 8).

theology have been constructed in the past (1992: 2) it is now necessary to recognize that literature might offer theology its best, perhaps only, chance to cease from the futile theodical exercises through which it has sought to extricate itself from the guilt of genocide and open itself and embrace that which it continually flees. For theology this would be both an end and a beginning. 'But that means bearing to think the unthinkable: embodying in textuality the unbearable so that embodiment and incarnation endures and embraces its own fragmentation and dismemberment' (1993: 161).

A book is not a body

This essay has employed an analysis of the gendered assumptions concerning the relation of literature and theology to explore three ways in which the disciplines are related, implicitly or explicitly, in contemporary debate.

It is clear that very significant issues are being negotiated under cover of what might be dismissed as a strictly academic concern: 'how do we study literature and theology?' Questions emerge which lie at the heart of what it means to articulate faith in the contemporary context. However, these issues are framed heuristically – and we should not lose sight of this fact. A book is not a body; a book is not a girl – really. And yet ... When we interrogate theoretical discourse with an awareness of how power is gendered in our culture, we can sometimes discern with greater clarity the high stakes which are being wagered in our academic exchanges.

Chapter 4

Fireflies and the Art Candle

Ienjoy my work. I consider it a huge privilege to enter each morning through the impressive gates of an ancient university and climb the steep stairs to my attic office overlooking the Memorial Chapel and Professors' Square. Here religion and learning have been prized for more than 500 years and as I teach, research and reflect upon literature and theology I am profoundly grateful for the academic inheritance which I can confidently and comfortably claim as my own.

But I live and work in one of the poorest cities in Europe. Poverty in this place can be measured brutally by counting the lost years of life[1] of those for whom the university in the midst of this city is a closed institution. You can differentiate the academic staff and students from the porters and cleaners who work here, by height alone. This is a visible daily reminder of the savage inequality which breeds in this place. It is a token of the many ethical dilemmas that face the person who has chosen to devote their energies to academic work. These challenges are particularly evident when the subject of your studies appears to be of little practical value. I am not working on cold fusion or a cure for cancer. So I must ask myself: in such a world as this, what is the cost of my entering through these gates and climbing these stairs and looking out of my window?

When I ponder these things I am disturbed by a memory. I was 18 years old and being interviewed for a place at university. Nothing in my previous experience had prepared me for the dim, book-lined study, for the urbane, cultivated and slightly cynical accent of the professor, for the dusty crystal decanter on his desk and the delicately stalked, intricately etched, half-full glass beside it. The professor was enjoying himself in

---

[1]   In Glasgow the average life expectancy is 70. For those who live in the poorest parts of the city it is 54. It is 75 in the United Kingdom overall.

teasing out the hopes and visions of a moderately attractive, very ideal-
istic but hopelessly immature applicant desperately confused about her
own calling. 'My dear,' he said to me, 'what possible earthly use is literature? Isn't it best to admit that *we* who love her,' his gesture here was both
inclusive and deeply compromising, 'have abandoned the barricades for
the boudoir?' I did not understand very much of what he went on to say
but I carried away with me a strong sense that I had been warned by a
middle-aged Don Juan about the dangers of seduction.

Invisible writing

Obviously I ignored the warning, but I have never been able to forget it.
   The essays I have drawn together in this book clearly demonstrate how
my work has been haunted by the challenge he articulated. 'What earthly
use is literature?' is a question that has been widely debated and to which
I shall return in the second part of this chapter. However, the same
question could equally be posed to other forms of writing which do not
employ the empirical and realistic conventions that would tie them to the
'real world'. Theology clearly stands as one of these and I shall begin by
examining some of the ways in which theologians have addressed this
same question.
   Or not! For many theologians appear unconcerned about the social
impact of their discourse. Perhaps, to function at all, we require a certain
amount of resilience to such distracting questions as, 'Does my work really
matter?' We pursue an activity that academic colleagues generally regard
as both archaic and arcane – a view shared by most members of the faith
communities we fondly believe we are addressing. For some of us, this
means that we can carry on business as usual, in the way that theologians
and religious philosophers have always done – that is, as if our mandate
was issued by God Almighty and the red wax, seals and ribbons that
adorn this ancient document ensure its validity for all time. I will never
forget the shock and revulsion I experienced on first reading Alvin
Plantinga's *God, Freedom, and Evil* (1974). In this 'classic text' he
patiently addresses the 'big' theological question, calmly concludes that
God can be understood as omniscient, omnipotent and morally perfect,
and issues these words of comfort to the perplexed: 'The existence of God
is neither precluded or rendered improbable by the existence of evil. Of
course, suffering and misfortune may nonetheless constitute a problem
for the theist; but the problem is not that his [sic] beliefs are logically or
probabilistically incompatible' (1974: 63). Perhaps few of us writing
today would use Plantinga's style or tone, but many would express the
same sentiments in softer sentences secure in confidence that our
knowledge of the truth of God (who is, thankfully, omniscient,
omnipotent and morally perfect) justifies the value of our endeavours –

even if others, whose vision may be sadly obscured by suffering and misfortune, cannot see this.

Of course, not all theologians would assume such aloof perspectives and certainly since the emergence of liberation theology in the 1970s very many theologians have argued vociferously that the question of human suffering (and now also ecological travail) determines the theological agenda of our age. I am happy to align myself with this position but, sadly, it does not resolve my ethical dilemmas. The problem, it seems to me, is that whilst lip service is paid to the importance of orthopraxis (as opposed to orthodoxy), for most of us *writing* about transformation displaces other forms of engagement. In other words, we employ the discourse of political activism as if that constituted in itself political action. There are some notable, and high-profile, theologians who do pursue a dual path. They write liberating theology and they act in the cause of liberation. However, for most of us (with kids, local commitments, books to write, bills to pay, etc.) this is an occasional occurrence[2] rather than a habit of life. Our *writing* is our most significant contribution to the world but we connive to disguise this. The rhetorical strategy we employ to do so is *either* subtly to imply that our writing gains its validity because it springs from our (more important) committed action *or* to suggest it is significant because it is resourcing other people of faith to undertake transformative action themselves. Frequently both premises are assumed to work together. The writing links the author and reader in a line of communication that (it is implied) springs from and results in faithful action but it is not in itself liberating; having done its self-effacing work the writing 'disappears'. It is merely functional and strategic, without potency in its own right. Our uneasiness that we might not be doing what we should be doing with our time and energy is concealed in this vanishing trick of writing.

Although it is important to distinguish the first position from the second (which can still justifiably claim to be wrestling faithfully with issues that really matter to people), what unites them both is that the writing itself is not considered significant. For theologians who view themselves as communicators of eternal truths the main concern is to transmit these in the clearest form possible. Their work is a mirror to the divine reality; it does not shine with its own light. For the second group of theologians, what happens off the page is of infinitely greater significance than what is written on it. My proficient readers will recognize that when an author neatly divides up the world into two distinct parts, as I

---

[2]   Of course most theologians operating from this perspective are people of goodwill who would rise to meet the challenge of the hour; making public interventions and aligning themselves with progressive causes when necessity forces them to do so and regularly paying their party dues. However, this is very different from an activist lifestyle which is not easily accommodated within the demands of a teaching programme, the struggle for tenure and the requirement to publish.

have done here, they can confidently expect to encounter a third way.
There exists another group of theologians, diverse in their outlooks and
opinions, who are very concerned indeed with what happens in religious
writing.

Contagious words

Amongst these a few names stand out. Gordon Kaufman is well known
for his efforts (for example, 1993a; 1993b; 1995) to reconstruct the
Christian tradition and for the challenge he repeatedly articulates to
other theologians that they apply themselves to the deliberate production
of more ethically acceptable God language that will overcome the social
conservatism generated by the symbolism we currently employ. For him
rewriting theology is in itself an act of resistance to the oppressive forces
that conscript religious idioms to sustain their power. What he sometimes
refers to as 'the symbol "God"' has been used to sustain a cosmic hierarchical pattern which 'provided the basis for similar hierarchical patterns
in human affairs; those who are male/white/wealthy/powerful determine
the order to which those who are female/black/poor/weak must submit'
(1993b: 106). Reappraising and revisioning 'this symbol can focus in a
powerful way our attention and devotion and lives ... on those dimensions of the ecological and historical order in which we live that facilitate
our moving further ... towards attaining our full humanity' (1993b:
113).[3]

Sallie McFague has pursued a pioneering path from her analysis of the
'world shattering'[4] effects of parabolic utterance to her work on
metaphorical theology and more latterly the creative employment of
new metaphors which implicate Christian understandings of the divine
in practices of ecological justice (1993). Rebecca Chopp has engaged
perhaps more than any other feminist theologian with the question of
whether linguistic changes impact upon social structures. In her earlier
writing she affirms that the cultural work of symbolic transformation and
activist politics are both necessary and important – although the latter
appears more important than the first. In later writing the two are more
closely integrated. She enthusiastically affirms the political importance of

---

[3]   I am sceptical that the tradition can be as painlessly reimagined as Kaufman
appears to imply. Perhaps his view that theology is a straightforwardly human
construction that is overdue for renovation is one that I do not find does justice to the
stubborn traces of alterity that reside within religious language.

[4]   A claim made on behalf of parables by John Crossan (1975) whose work
comparing myth and parables was generative of much key thinking in this area. See
Winquist (1995: 76).

narrativity (1995) and the crucial role a poetics of testimony[5] might play in the construction of a new social imaginary (2001).[6] Theology, with other forms of discursive practice, has the potential to play an important role in this work of cultural transformation.

Both McFague and Chopp stand broadly within the traditions of feminist liberation theology but they have ventured into the dangerous territory of literary theory to find resources for their reflection upon theological writing – although this is by no means an unproblematic step for members of the women's guild. There are other male theologians who have enthusiastically embraced poststructuralist theory and have come to see the process of inscribing the name of God as in itself a destabilizing and disruptive act. Amongst these the work of John Caputo,[7] who has written on the poetics of obligation (1993) as well as on the process of divine invocation (2006), stands out for its deep appreciation of the creative potential of genre disruption in philosophical and religious thinking. Charles Winquist is similarly concerned with the destabilizing effects of writing the name of God and offers some of the most sustained and interesting contemporary reflections upon theological writing.

In *Desiring Theology* (1995), Winquist self-consciously assumes the mantle of Paul Tillich: the theologian who, in opposition to current notions of orthodoxy, has come to represent the requirement to take culture with utmost seriousness when articulating theology. Tillich's work belongs to more confident times when it was still possible to think of the theologian providing answers to the 'deep' questions posed by culture. In these less certain days, Winquist proposes that we see theology as a discursive practice (*as writing*) which differs from others in that it breaks the frame of normal utterance. Applying Deleuze's notion of the singularity, 'singularities are turning points and points of inflection; bottlenecks, knots, foyers, and centres; points of fusion, condensation and boiling points; points of tears and joy; sickness and health, hope and anxiety, "sensitive points"' (Deleuze, in Winquist, 1995: 48), he asks whether in our own context there is a 'singularity about speaking or writing the name of God?' (1995: 85). The effect of this utterance is not, as it might have been in the past, to make a direct intervention that transforms dominant discourse but rather to taint, infect or pollute such discourse, thus

---

[5]   A concept developed from her engagement with the work of Shoshona Felman, a literary critic who has herself reflected deeply on the political implications of her own academic practice (see Felman and Laub 1992).

[6]   See Charles Taylor (2004) for a discussion of the social imaginary. Taylor focuses upon the way people imagine their social surroundings 'in images, stories and legends … the social imaginary is that common understanding that makes possible common practices and widely shared sense of legitimacy' (2004: 23).

[7]   Who would probably resist my designation of his work as theological – but I hope will forgive and understand.

rendering it corrupted from within. Theology comprises 'texts that are unsafe and are a contagion that makes all texts unsafe' (1995: 129). The glorious science without content, the grammar of non-existing entities, destabilize other forms of speech which, when placed in relation to it, see their own foundations melt into air. Theology in this perspective becomes a transient and homeless discourse which 'inhabits the edges and cracks of the dominant culture. It is a nomad discipline wandering, wondering and erring' (1995: 133)[8] and the theologian has a modest but also a vital role to play. In the 'ever unsettled reality of text production ... [t]here are always spaces, discursive and nondiscursive spaces, that although they are not sanctioned or proper to a dominant discourse can be inhabited by theological interrogations. I am suggesting that theology can insinuate itself into dominant culture' (1995: 133).

I am attracted to Winquist's diffident vision of the potentially transformative impact of theological writing. His modest approach is appropriate to the paradoxical situation in which we now find ourselves. Theology can no longer lay claim to being the Queen of Sciences – and I regard this as a largely positive thing. But it is also the case that there is more interest in theology today than there has been for many years and, no longer effectively contained, it has effected a seepage and contagion which has stained and infected the work of many contemporary thinkers.[9]

Alongside other theologians, such as those mentioned above, Winquist offers an encouraging picture of theological writing performing a leavening action in cultural terms. By focusing upon questions such as 'What cultural disruption does writing the name of God produce?' they are attempting to offer a genuinely theological response to the question of why their writing matters. However, in focusing upon symbols, metaphors, parables and poesis they are also implicitly reframing the theological tradition as a literary inheritance and, as I have already stated, it is a characteristic feature of the reflections of such theologians upon theological writing that they draw deeply upon contemporary literary theory to sustain their claims. For these theologians theology matters in a similar way that literature matters and so it is to debates upon the politics of 'poetics' that I now turn. Interestingly, we shall discover as this discussion progresses that, while theologians are using literary theory to explore the importance of theological writing, this body of theory itself has taken a decidedly theological turn.

---

[8]   Winquist draws deeply upon Mark C. Taylor's (1984) work but his approach is rather different. Graham Ward identifies Winquist as representing a more complex and respectful attitude to theism (Ward 2005: 327) than that of many other postmodern theologians and atheologians.

[9]   Derrida would be an obvious example but to that list we could add Kristeva, Irigaray, Cixous and more recently Judith Butler. There are other significant contemporary thinkers such as Paul Ricoeur, Emmanuel Levinas and Gillian Rose whose theological interests and affiliations are not in question.

Militant aesthetics

The work of Paul Ricoeur provides one of the most important resources for those who would argue that literature has political significance. At the centre of his thinking is the claim that through metaphoric utterance we do not merely describe what exists or communicate our experience; we create and recreate the world. The metaphor accomplishes this as it brings together previously unrelated elements in an act of semantic innovation. As Mario Valdes puts this, when 'two energies converge' they open up 'an unknown referential field within language' (1991: 14). This sends fissures and cracks through the surface of the known world we currently inhabit. Ricoeur argues that this brings down the fragile shelters we have built to stabilize our lives and changes 'our way of dwelling in the world ... metaphor shatters not only the previous structures of our language but also the previous structures of what we call reality .... With metaphor we experience the metamorphosis of language and reality' (1991: 85).

In Ricoeur's thinking this image of the metaphor, as the place where impossible elements combine to generate creative energy, comes to represent what can be achieved through literature and imaginative thinking. There are those who believe that the greatest contribution literature can make is to reveal the reality of human life with greater clarity. George Newlands, for example, celebrates the 'what literature does best', namely presenting 'a critically realist account of human life as it actually is' (2004: 118).[10] Ricoeur takes a contradictory approach. What literature does best is to open us to what does not exist, what is not true and what has not yet been thought. As extended metaphoric utterance literature has a world-destroying and world-creating function. Precisely because the literary work *is* illusion, artifice, fiction, not what it appears to be – the more valuable the function it fulfils as a probe, a means of night vision and a passageway between alternate worlds. There is nothing apologetic in the claims that Ricoeur makes for the political power of fiction:

The more imagination deviates from that which is called reality in ordinary vision the more it approaches the heart of reality which is no longer the world of manipulable objects, but the world into which we have been thrown by birth and within which we try to orient ourselves by projecting our innermost possibilities upon it ... Under the shock of fiction reality becomes problematic for us. We attempt to elude this painful situation by

---

[10]   Although elsewhere in his work Newlands affirms the importance of 'the power of metaphor, which moves from the literal towards an openness towards the unfamiliar' (2004: 51). As he would be likely to maintain, these two appraisals of literature are not necessarily contradictory.

putting beyond criticism a concept of reality according to which the 'real' is what our everyday interests project upon the horizon of the world. (1991: 133)

In this frame literature is always shaking the scaffolding supporting everyday life and this enables him to affirm that 'our aesthetical grasping of the world is a militant understanding' (1991: 117). Richard Kearney describes this 'militant aesthetics' as a means of producing 'imaginative variations of the world, thereby offering us the freedom, to conceive of the world in new ways and engage in action which might lead to its trans-formation' (2004: 41–2).

Impossible space

The work of Ricoeur on metaphor has been interpreted not only as spanning the divide between the world of the text and the material world of human action, but also as pointing towards a liminal space in language and textuality in which extraordinary things can happen. The rich image of the metaphor, which incorporates differences without domination, has been credited with restoring to us a primordial world in which the divide that currently exists between subject and object is overcome.[11] This separation is the result of attempts to gain mastery both of our own disordered subjectivity and the world around us. Ricoeur argues that poetic language 'restores to us participation-in or belonging-to an order of things which precedes our capacity to oppose ourselves to things taken as objects opposed to a subject' (Ricoeur, in McIntosh 1998: 132). In other words the metaphor does not allow passive manipulation; it confronts and involves us, 'detaching us from the process of knowing by objectifying and moving one toward a process of knowing by self-bestowal and participation' (Ricoeur, in McIntosh 1998: 132). The metaphor draws us into an encounter with that which it manifests. We are not pointed towards a fact or proposition; we are confronted with something closer to a revelation or epiphany.

Thus the metaphor, as a site of a meeting which defies the subject/object order of the regulated world, can also been interpreted as the space in which we are enabled to make a privileged encounter with alterity. Ricoeur is not alone amongst contemporary theorists in his fascination with the disruption that poetic language represents in a symbolic order

---

[11] This is a subject explored extensively in the work of psychoanalytical theorists such as Julia Kristeva. She also credits poetic language with the ability to traverse the thetic divide between the maternal sphere of undifferentiated jouissance and the paternal sphere of language.

that is predicated upon the banishment of the Other from representation.[12] Julia Kristeva, for example, takes as a major focus within her oeuvre the way in which poetic language embodies that which is repressed in the achievement of subjectivity (our ecstatic union with the Other, our bodily desires, our indiscreet sensations, our sense of things beyond language, all that is 'feminine' in an order based upon the word of the father) and carries its destructive and regenerative power into the realm of language and culture:

> the aesthetic task – a descent into the foundations of the symbolic construct – amounts to retracing the fragile limits of the speaking being, closest to its dawn ... 'subject' and 'object' push each other away, confront each other, collapse, and start again – inseparable, contaminated, condemned, at the boundary of what is assimilable, thinkable: abject. Great modern literature unfolds over that terrain: Dostoevsky, Lautreamont, Proust, Artaud, Kafka, Celine. (1982: 18)

In later works she describes her lifelong quest 'to see how far literature could go as a journey to the end of night, the end of the limit of meaning' (2000: 112). In these recent texts literature is frequently evoked in quasi-mystical terms as 'thought of the impossible, or perhaps, literature as a-thought' (2000: 113).[13]

In such passages Kristeva expresses the conviction, which theological readings of Ricoeur's work also point us towards, that what is happening in the processes that constitute poetic language can appropriately be described as the encroachment of sacred into a world which fears its ambivalent power. This is a powerful but not a new insight. In his remarkable speech on the work of poetry and the nature of art (delivered in 1960 and published as 'The Meridian' in 1978) the poet Paul Celan explores the same ideas in terms that have a remarkably contemporary feel. He argues that poetry is concerned to articulate what is normally silenced, or which takes the breath away. It makes its testimony on behalf of that which is alien to language and that which culture would rather dispose of and forget. In similar terms to Kristeva, Celan associates that which is abjected in this way with the sacred:

> But I think – and this thought can scarcely come as a surprise to you – I think that it has always belonged to the expectations of the poem, in

[12] I have phrased this concern in 'Lacanian' terms but the phallogocentric nature of discourse is not only significant within psychoanalytic theory but is widely assumed within Derridean and Foucauldian analyses and within all forms of feminist poststructuralism.

[13] Kristeva's use of mystical and sublime discourse in these texts should not be read as implying an orthodox religious faith. Her interest in the sacred has other roots.

precisely this manner to speak in the cause of the strange – no, I can no
longer use this word – in precisely this manner to speak *in the cause of an
Other* – who knows, perhaps in the cause of a *wholely Other*. (1978: 35–6)

And like Ricoeur he celebrates the potential that the poem presents to re-
enter a primordial world in which the subject/object divide that sustains
the factuity of everyday life is set aside and another form of knowledge
is revealed '*in the mystery of an encounter*' (1978: 37). It is the poet's duty
to locate the place in which this meeting might happen and guide others
towards it:

> I am also seeking the point of my own origin since I have once again arrived
> at my point of departure.
> I am seeking all of that on the map with a finger which is uncertain, because
> it is restless – on a child's map, as I readily confess.
> None of these places are to be found, they do not exist, but I know where
> they would have to exist – above all at the present time – and … I find
> something …
> I find something which binds and which, like the poem leads to an
> encounter. (1978: 40)

As a poet-witness to the Shoah, Celan's reference to encountering 'the
Other' can be read at a number of levels and certainly includes reference
to the multidinous 'others' whom history has silenced. There now exists
a significant body of writing upon the manner in which literature is able
to witness to trauma in a way that is impossible within the confines of
normal everyday discourse (see pages 45–8). In so doing it fulfils the
crucial political role of remembering, witnessing or bearing testimony.
Theodor Adorno, having famously despaired of the morality of artistic
endeavour after Auschwitz, later came to believe that 'politics has
migrated into … art'(2000: 318). In other words it was only through
what he termed 'autonomous art' (which we can understand as art that
is concerned primarily with its own authenticity in contrast to art with a
political mission) that we can articulate the inexpressible nature of
contemporary historical events and the obligations these place upon us.
    It is interesting to note that the philosophers, psychoanalysts and poets
considered above find it necessary to use sublime language in order to
describe their understanding of the political impact of literary writing.
Even the most level-headed of cultural critics find they cannot describe
the significance of extra-ordinary utterance without recourse to such
terms themselves. Homi Bhabha, for example, describes how when critics
reach towards an understanding of the social significance of literature (its
'worlding') they experience the unworlding of their own disciplinary
conventions.

If we are seeking a 'worlding' of literature, then perhaps it lies in a critical act that attempts to grasp the sleight of hand with which literature conjures with historical specificity, using the medium of psychic uncertainty, aesthetic distancing, or the obscure signs of the spirit-world, the sublime and the subliminal. As literary creatures and political animals we ought to concern ourselves with the understanding of human action and the social world as a moment when *something is beyond control, but is not beyond accommodation.* This act of writing the world, of taking the measure of its dwelling, is magically caught in Morrison's description of her house of fiction – art as 'the fully realized presence of a haunting' of history. Read as an image that describes the relation of art to social reality, my translation of Morrison's phrase becomes a statement on the political responsibility of the critic. For the critic must attempt to fully realize, and take responsibility for, the unspoken, unrepresented pasts that haunt the historical present. (1994: 12)

Faith after theory?

The writers I have briefly discussed above together contribute to an understanding of literature as a form of utterance that is deeply political and most particularly so when it attends to its own concerns rather than allies itself with a cause or ideology. Do I wish that I could travel back in time and use my new knowledge of the work of these thinkers to make a better response to the challenge that was put to me so many years ago? It would be very nice to confront the cynical professor with the combined weight of Adorno, Ricoeur, Kristeva et al. and speak to him eloquently of the 'world shattering potential' of an encounter with alterity as it is presented in the literary text. I couldn't do it then. I could do it now. But somehow I don't think I would convince him – and perhaps the reason is because I do not think he was entirely wrong in his descriptions of the seduction of literature.

I love to read the arguments I have rehearsed above. There is a special quality to texts that emerge from contexts in which normal discourse fractures and this makes them particularly rewarding to study. I am fascinated by the way in which the concerns of literary and theological writing converge over the contested terrain of politics and this is one of the most interesting aspects of borderland research. However, I am still confronted with the everyday reality of this intractably awful world and cannot say with confidence that the assertions that are made on behalf of literary and theological writing can be *easily* sustained within it. Can they be sustained at all?

In these chastened times, 'after theory', the claims of poststructuralism concerning the political potential of semantic innovation are more frequently challenged. Jonathan Culler, for example, in his contribution to the important collection *What's Left of Theory* (Butler, Guillory and Thomas 2000), argues that we are losing faith in arguments that optimistically assume the transformative potential of literary texts. He states that confidence in linguistic innovation should now be replaced by a more modest assessment of the potential of literature to help us 'stage' (rehearse) our own sense of agency and develop an empathetic awareness of those who are unlike us:

> But there are probably few of us left in theory who will be surprised or annoyed by the conclusion that literature does not necessarily have moral and political benefits: arguments for the disruptive and emancipatory value of the avant-garde can always be countered – we know this only too well – by claims about the normalising and policing functions of literary scenarios … [it] has been the tendency in recent thinking about literature to relate the defence of the literary and the specificity thereof not to questions of the distinctiveness of literary language or to the radical potential of the disruption of meanings but to the staging of agency on the one hand and to engagements with otherness on the other. (Culler 2000: 280)

I do not wish to join Culler in repudiating the radical claims that have been made for literature as a force for change. I think his assertion that there are few true believers left is an exaggeration; a swing of the pendulum, perhaps, away from too great a faith in the power of imagining. However, the strong case he makes here for recognizing literature as an ambivalent force seems to me incontrovertible. The champions of the political efficacy of literature sometimes appear too eager to tame the wanton and enrol her in the cause of social reform. This is one of the chief problems I have with their writing. Ricoeur is a fundamentally optimistic theorist whose confidence in the illuminative powers of imagination is rarely shaken by the shades that inhabit the literary realm. Kristeva celebrates the power of literature to shake the symbolic order but does not offer an ethical critique of the pornographic, anti-semitic and sadistic content of much of the avant-garde literature she champions. Adorno's comments on the political salvation promised in autonomous art should not be allowed to pass without recognition that there is little evidence to support his claim that Kafka's political influence has been greater than the ideologically committed 'realism' of Brecht (see Adorno 2000: 306–18).[14] Celan's moving defence of poetry cannot be read without an awareness that this is a statement of faith made on the edge of despair – a despair that led him to mutilate his own work and in the end overwhelmed him. Perhaps this is why it is necessary for him, and other literary critics who employ the

---

[14]   Indeed realism cannot be easily dismissed as a reactionary form of writing as has been commonly assumed by many poststructuralist theorists.

same gesture, to use the language of the sublime (theology) to describe their defiant hope that poetry speaks in the cause of the Other? The claim cannot easily be made in a mundane tongue.

I think it is best to admit quite frankly that choosing writing is a dreadfull decision that is always made with an awareness of unfulfilled responsibilities and the neglect of other calls and obligations. I would also describe it as an act of love and faith in the possibility that following our desires might, inadvertently, lead us to a place where love, politics and mystery are reunited. This is a perspective that is powerfully articulated in the work of Hélène Cixous.

The possibility of love

In *Hélène Cixous Rootprints* (1997), an intensely personal book in which she reviews the concerns that have dominated her writing career, Cixous states, 'The ethical question of politics has always haunted me, as I imagine it haunts all fireflies drawn to the art-candle' (1997: 6). This image of the flame and the firefly graphically conveys the lure of writing and the strong possibility that fireflies, such as myself, will always choose it – despite, not because of, the political concerns that trouble our sleep. Throughout her oeuvre Cixous chooses metaphors of desire and temptation to convey her sense that placing faith in writing is never a straightforward good. It always entails a fall from innocence. We are: 'always on the trail of the first of all human stories, the story of *Eve and the Apple* ... The stakes are extremely simple, it is a question of the apple, does one eat it or not? Will one enter into contact with the intimate inside of the fruit or not?' (1988: 15). This choice, 'Eat the fruit or not?' is the theme of an important but neglected early work *To Live the Orange* (1979). In this Cixous uses the orange as a metaphor for the vivid and enticing, fleshly fruit of writing. She has resolved to enjoy the sensuous pleasures of devouring it. However, her delight is curtailed because the phone keeps ringing demanding she take action on behalf of women suffering oppression in Iran. Orange/Iran – which takes precedence. Desire or duty? Or is there a link between the two: 'Under what conditions could a woman say, without dying of shame ... *"the love of the orange is political too"* – at what cost?' (1979: 26).

There is no easy answer to this question. It is a scandal and should be acknowledged as such. The woman who grasps the orange does not, through so doing, send medical aid to suffering women, she does not restore to them lost civil rights. What she does is seize what this world denies and enjoys it, now and right here in the midst of pain and violence. She declares herself an initiate, a believer 'in the possibility of love; and a link between this "libido of the other" and writing' (1989: 109). She also dares to offer this as 'the present of a living rose, so that the infinite tenderness contained in a rose may through the forty sadnesses reach veiled women' (1979: 100). What Cixous is reaching towards here is a view of writing as consummated love in the midst of the most appalling circumstances enabling us to contemplate being fully 'contemporaneous with a living rose and with concentration camps' (1979: 100).

This is a peculiar inversion of the myth of the Fall. It is through eating the forbidden fruit that we are able to enter Paradise. This is a world 'contemporaneous' with our own but not functioning according to the law. In it we can embrace the Other, receive the dead again and enjoy our freedom. Gaining access to these precious fruits is of course forbidden and with just cause:

> We recognize the old grandiose and threatening hymn: you will not drink, you will not eat, you will not read, you will not write, otherwise you will die.
> And they call reading a sin, and writing is a crime.
> And no doubt this is not entirely false.
> They will never forgive us for this Somewhere Else. (1993: 26)

In this 'Somewhere Else' we can enjoy 'eating the forbidden fruit, making forbidden love, changing eras, changing families, changing destinies and changing day for night' (1993: 21). In Cixous' early works this enjoyment is imaged as an erotic passion that sustains lovers in the midst of war (1990 [1975]; 1982). In later texts, the love is reimaged as the deeper longing we have for the lost, the dead, for the beloved child. In whatever frame it is pictured it is a transgressive love that is always shame-cheeked. We cannot conceal the fact that our lips and hands are stained with goblin juices. The claim that we are keeping the door of Paradise open for others to enter can always be challenged by those who would rather we stood side by side with them in the streets. But perhaps we have another response to make.

Politics cannot change day to night, restore the dead, breathe life into the still child. Whatever future reformations we might achieve in our social arrangements, politics will never achieve these goals and this results in the cycles of hope and disillusionment that always accompany political movements. Furthermore in politics vision always succumbs to bureaucracy, cruelty is first an instrument and then a way of life. Politics does not have the strength it needs *alone* to transform the world. I would not claim, as others have done, that literature does the work of politics; it is rather that politics needs the Somewhere Else of writing to partner and provoke it. They can stand together at the barricades and explore the secret intimacies of the boudoir. So let us admit that writing is 'often inadmissible, contrary, terribly dangerous and risks turning into complacency' (Cixous 1993: 13) but it does have the power to bring armfuls of roses to the condemned.

Chapter 5

The Wisdom of Sheba and Fictions of Faith

I lived my childhood in a strange fantasy land inhabited by Amazons who were pirates and camped on Wild Cat Island; the O'Sullivan Twins who were boarders at St Clare's and ate anchovy paste sandwiches without crusts; and Anne of Green Gables who was always cheerful because somebody sent her crutches in a barrel (!) when she was very young. Alongside these characters dwelt a host of others, some even more odd and exotic, who had come alive from the pages of my *Illustrated Children's Bible*. This was given to me as a present for being Shirley and Arnold's bridesmaid – despite the fact that I had my heart set on a stuffed Spanish donkey like the one Shirley had brought home from Lloret de Mar.

I often think the fact that my first Bible was big, red and full of pictures rather than small and black and full of writing, has decisively influenced my life. It has fed my religious imagination. In this chapter much of what I write refers back to the story of Solomon's famous judgement (1 Kgs 3.16–27). Whenever I think about this narrative I find myself transported back into the heavy, colourful pages of that fascinating book. I see a hall of fine pillars and I watch as courtiers stare aghast at a king (naked to the waist and with gold bands round each wrist – but not bald like Yul Brynner) who holds a tiny baby in one hand and a huge scimitar in the other.

This is Solomon the wise one.

And this is a terrifying scene.

It fascinated and appalled me then. It haunts and disturbs me now. The heat of the moment, the small mewing cries of the baby. Solomon who thinks he understands the women lying prostrate before him – but he does not! The violence and the awful, simple vision of the truth. For me this compelling image has come to represent my own relation to the sacred tradition I teach and preach.

In this chapter I 'come out' as someone who not only reflects upon literature and theology but who also 'performs' sacred words. I am a preacher. I don't just read stories; I write and speak them. The literary, theological and critical texts I work with are ingested and rearticulated in the form of sermons. The role and persona of 'the preacher' is one that many religious feminists struggle with (see Durber 2007). There are powerful rules and conventions which structure the practice of preaching in ways that run contrary to many of our cherished political commitments. And yet, it is my experience that the pulpit is a rare and sacred space within our culture[1] in which the performance of sacramental narratives, traditionally staged only by men, can produce extraordinary results. This essay is a reflection upon the act of preaching; preaching out of love and faith – but without innocence.

I have structured my thoughts around a midrash which represents much of what I understand preaching 'as a woman' to entail. My midrash twines and curls around a sacred story and engages with the forceful conventions, silences and gaps upon which the older text is established. Midrash is an appealing vehicle for feminists who cherish their religious identity but also wish to argue with it and re-vision it. We have freely adapted the potential of this Jewish tradition, in which the scriptural narratives become the starting point for debate, a forum for personal reflections and the inspiration for new stories which begin at the point where the authoritative text leaves off.[2] In creating this story I have drawn upon midrashic traditions that imply a passionate relationship between Solomon and the Queen of Sheba. I have found they allow me to express the ambivalent passion I feel for preaching. Sheba also gives me a narrative voice that has its own power and is capable of speaking out against the authority of the king.[3]

Sheba's story

I am treated like a king. There is sherbet and dancing and golden bowls of sweet wine and fine, clever conversation between Solomon and me. And

---

[1]   For a very interesting discussion of the impact preaching can make see Robinson 2005b: 227–44.

[2]   Jewish feminists have been particularly active in the creation of midrash but have encouraged other women of faith to exploit this strategy in relation to their own traditions. See Alicia Ostriker (1993; 1997) and Plaskow (1990).

[3]   There is no biblical warrant for my decision to imagine the queen as present at the famous judgement scene. However, it is my conviction that the dark figure of female wisdom is always present at crucial events such as this and she may offer a very different verdict upon circumstances as they unfold.

then the two women enter and I am still, of course, seated on a throne next to Solomon's, but somehow I am also bowed down on the ground as they are. I sense their fear, the heat of their fear, and fear of the child. They have called me out of myself to share their suffering. Two street women and two children. One small one crying out to me and the other baby blue and still – speaking only with silence. They are demanding that I step down from my pedestal.

He was too quick, Solomon. He did not pause to ask one question. How came you to your wretched house? To the childbed without the help of midwives? What weight upon your heart made your sleep so heavy that it crushed out the breath of your baby? Whose face did the child have? Some man from one night only? A childhood sweetheart stolen from you? Or maybe it was a brother perhaps, a father or an uncle? A familiar face, unwelcome at the breast?

Solomon was too quick to beckon to a soldier. His gaze was on me. The show was partly for my benefit. He snatched the child and held that great sword over its poor little body and he did not look the women in the eyes, or he would have seen what I saw:

The sudden fear of one woman. Oh, I did not foresee that it would come to this. I cannot carry my deception through this far. Yes. I took her child. Yes, because my baby was so still and it would not suck. The living child with its hungry lips seemed to offer relief but I could not have kept it long, only a little while. I would have confessed to her and perhaps she could have forgiven. I would have shared as a sister does in the raising of the child. *'Give it back to her, don't kill her baby.'*

And the other woman. Feverish from the childbed, in pain and her full breasts swollen, but in her passion she defies him. How many other men had stood over her with violent hand held high? How many times had she seen the manicured hands of wealth and power strike life from the bodies of those she loved? Does the wise king not know that sometimes mothers do kill their own children, when love burns like fire or when the times are too hard for the little ones to bear? Well, mighty Solomon, God's own anointed one, dare you do with your own hand what your servants do on your behalf far away from the laughter and the splendour of this court? Will you make great your reputation at the cost of one more small victim? She burned with defiance as she said, *'Yes, Oh King. Cut the child in two.'*

He made a hasty judgement, and a wrong one. But then, how could he have done otherwise? Did not God himself smite down the first child his mother bore to David? Was not the beautiful Bathsheba torn apart between two men? Her husband, her king, her husband. The king killed her husband and the king became her husband. Was not she cut in pieces with one baby silent and still and another crying and crying? Solomon does not dare enquire too deeply into the secrets of a mother's love.

He has made his judgement and so the women must leave. I feel compelled to follow them. I detain the one whose proud heart and arms are empty. '*Wait a little while.*' I have sent servants and they return with the small, still bundle. The forgotten, silent child. I have called for one of Solomon's golden bowls and in it we pour fresh water. We unwrap the swaddling bands from the small body, full term and so thin, hungry even in the womb. Tenderly we wash the baby and we both weep although we did not carry or bear him. The other woman has taken away the living child and left her precious baby in our care. We are the mothers of the dead. We wash his sweet little body and uncurl his small fingers.

We name the child with a name. It is the name Solomon was given as a baby by the prophet Nathan when God announced that his anger against David was appeased and the little boy would be allowed to live. We name the dead child Jedidiah. It means 'beloved of God'. It is a name Solomon does not care to use as an adult – he does not wish to think in what manner he came by it ... We give the child that name and then we hold it and rock it for long hours; singing it sweet songs before we wrap it in rough linen and lay it in a cradle of earth.

A child runs through the corridors and plays in the courtyard of my palace. A bright child of laughter and delight. It is the child I bore of those nights of sherbet and sweet wine and good conversation with Solomon before the two women broke in upon that golden world and shattered it all in pieces. I have called the child after its father and after its poor brother: Jedidiah. With God's help I will lead it along a slow and gentle path, a winding, secret path, to wisdom. For it is said that wisdom is justified by her children.

Seated on a throne next to Solomon's

I can imagine the gorgeous couple, white robed, olive skinned, dark eyed. Their heads are close together; they are whispering words of wisdom to each other; complicit in their knowledge and understanding. Her throne is gold as his is but rather lower, a little narrower, set back slightly. Placed thus she frames and complements his greatness. She does not challenge or threaten him in any way.

Of course I know it is a great privilege to be a preacher. To mount up high, six feet above contradiction and look down in regal splendour. And I am aware that this privilege entails responsibility. The first responsibility is to abide by the rules. I was not *so* aware of this when I approached my minister one Sunday morning in the crowded church hall and casually announced that I wanted to train as a preacher.

He: Why?
Me: Because I have been coming to church for 17 years, since I was a baby. I've listened to hundreds of sermons and I think I can do it.

He: Think you can do it?

Me: Yes, and better than a lot of the people who do it now.

Don't try this.[4] It doesn't work. What you need to say first is, 'I really enjoyed your sermon.' The next phrase should begin something like, 'Unworthy as I am …'

The first rule of preaching is that you require authority to do it and that this authority has to come from somewhere else. It's not your pulpit, after all and, in the quaint, old phrase, the pulpit must be guarded. So where does this authority come from? First, of course, from the Church which, when you provide them with an appropriate version of your calling (not the one above), will decide within its councils whether or not to ratify this in the appropriate way. They will then train you in the required knowledge, techniques and etiquette. But that is not enough authority. Your authority must also come from the Word of God, not from your own eloquence, intelligence and reason. A great deal of twentieth-century theology (from Barth to Bultmann) is concerned with the mechanism through which text becomes Word and ancient historical narratives are transformed into *kerygma*. I have studied these and it seems to be a mysterious process of extraordinary transformation. But whatever route you imagine 'the Word' taking into life the text itself is always its necessary vehicle.

There are problems with both of these sources of authority for women. After all, they have conspired together for nearly two millennia to guard the pulpit against us. We face a complicated double bind when claiming our authority from these sources – two sources where it has been so emphatically denied. Of course, it is possible to avoid this problem by preaching as if you were a man. Women who wish to succeed in prominent positions of leadership frequently do so by supporting and conforming to male norms. If they do not choose this option, and set out as preachers to speak against the structures that have denied them voice, women must negotiate a mighty contradiction. We require official recognition and scriptural precedent to preach against the coercive power of the law and the letter.

Fortunately, we have recourse to another strategy which has proved effective since ancient times. We can appeal to the Spirit (who, happily, is a girl) as the source of our authority and power. This has been a favourite recourse for saints and mystics throughout the ages and continues to be effective today. In her hugely significant work, *Changing*

---

[4] Fortunately my minister was a gentle and helpful person who tactfully informed me that while he thought he understood the nature of my 'calling', the Local Preachers' Meeting probably would not. He advised me to go away and work on a more appropriate account of my vocation. It took me quite a while to get it right.

the Subject (1994), Mary McClintock Fulkerson examines how Pentecostal women preachers in deeply conservative churches claim this source of legitimacy for their preaching. There are problems here too, however. This works best with impassioned, ecstatic, prophetic utterance. These can be accorded authority, but it is a different authority – that of the oracle, blind visionary or holy fool. Religious ecstasy can appear very close to madness. It seems the Holy Spirit of God prefers not to work from a written script (for the letter killeth and the Spirit giveth life) and if you are the type of preacher who does, this claim is not going to work so well for you.

But perhaps all this should not concern the woman preacher unduly. There is no point in searching endlessly for sources of authority when, whatever form we claim, our status is not going to be equal to that of our male colleagues. Her throne is gold as his but a little lower, a little narrower, slightly set back. Michèle le Doeuff, reflecting upon the very sophisticated registers of power that determine how voices are heard, argues that a woman speaking will not be accorded the same authority as a man – whatever her eloquence, intelligence or inspiration: 'The social importance crystallized around the speaker's name and the social values which govern reaction to the voice's timbre work together to form an unconscious hearing which hierarchizes individuals' utterances' (Le Doeuff 2002: 137). As those of us who preach will testify, despite modern techniques of amplification the most common comment women receive as they shake hands at the door is, 'I found it hard to hear you.' A true comment, I believe. There is something about a woman's public voice that is difficult to hear.

All this prompts me to conclude that, instead of asserting what we cannot achieve, women should bring into question the notion of authority as it commonly functions in preaching. Maybe we need to reframe this in terms of accountability? We could begin to ask ourselves the question that Adrienne Rich articulated not in terms of 'Where does my authority come from?' but rather, 'With whom do I cast my lot?'[5] Now, this question will inevitably lead us back to church and text and Spirit again, but by a different route. Raising it moves me to the next section of my midrash.

They have called me to share their suffering

I have already mentioned that the Church trains those it commissions to preach, and as part of my own training some fundamental principles were

---

[5]   A question that haunts her poetry. See her much-quoted reflections on this theme in 'Natural Resources', *The Dream of a Common Language*, 1978a: 60–7.

emphasized. One of the most important of these was that preaching should not be personal. Preachers should be very careful about using their own experience – or indeed any real person's experience! Most especially to be avoided was reference to aspects of life that people might find difficult, unfamiliar or distasteful. Those quaint books of sermon illustrations that novice preachers still purchase are full of stories of one-dimensional characters whose lives are remarkable only because of their great distance from our own. There are exceptions to this rule about referring to real people in their particularity and diversity. It is acceptable to talk about a few extra-special people but it helps if these are dead or foreign, and not overtly identified with one theological position. I have some suggestions here: Gladys Aylward, Dietrich Bonhoeffer, Nelson Mandela (strangely), Mother Teresa, Jean Vanier and St Francis of Assisi. These are all fine.

What these prohibitions against the particular (and we might also say against the embodied) amount to is the requirement that the preacher focus upon the universal truths of what the theologian David Tracy (1981) refers to as common human experience. The more general, the more 'true'. The more particular, the more subjective, the more 'false'. The problem with this position is that it tends towards abstraction, idealism and the unwitting reinscription of dominant cultural values – the voice of the disembodied universal is always the voice of the dominant male. As is frequently asserted by feminist and poststructuralist theorists alike, the view from nowhere is in fact always a view from somewhere and this somewhere is always the place of power, or to use that word again, authority. There are other views of how we might usefully come to understand, represent and speak the 'truths' of human existence. Significant in my own practice of preaching are three of these.

The first is the idea of situated knowledge (or standpoint epistemology). This affirms that how you see the world depends upon where you stand. The practical theologian Elaine Graham makes use of this principle in her important text *Making the Difference: Gender, Personhood and Theology* (1995). In this she dismisses the idea that women have a particular perspective on life because they speak directly from some genetically coded script. It is rather that having a woman's body places us in a particular cultural location which offers a distinctive vantage point from which to view experience. Graham draws upon work of the American theorist Donna Haraway to explore how women's viewpoints might become significant in re-forming pastoral practice:

> Haraway evokes the metaphor of vision – as embodied and situated. The idea of infinite vision, of seeing all in a universal or final perspective is plainly ridiculous, and to make such a claim is effectively to 'play God'. Thus an epistemology, modelled on the particularity and embodiment of all vision, comprises a 'usable but not innocent version of objectivity'.

This phrase 'usable but not innocent' has great potential. It means that we recognise the specificity of our knowing, the tentative and provisional nature of our claims to truth ... We can see bodies as 'vantage points' from which we advance hypotheses about the world, rather than ontological essences which make absolute claims about the nature of reality. At the same time the materiality of *situated knowledge* allows for a moral imperative because the knowledge clearly does have relevance to concrete human situations. (1995: 211)

The second idea is the argument that there exists within culture a mute zone, or a dark zone if you like, that is not the subject of public discourse for 'dominant groups control the forms or structures through which consciousness can be articulated' (Showalter 1986b: 262). This notion has been significant within feminist literary theory. Elaine Showalter, for example, employs anthropological tools to argue that non-dominant groups depend for their survival on the understanding they have of those who have power. A corresponding knowledge is not required of the dominant group. They do not need to enter into the eclipsed moon of experience that is particular to the less powerful – she calls this the wild zone.[6] In illustration of this concept we might think of the intimate knowledge black South African domestic workers possessed concerning every aspect of their employers' lives in apartheid South Africa. A reciprocal knowledge was not necessary for whites and, indeed, it would have been deeply disturbing for them to have approached the muted zone. Or we might think of the film *Gosford Park*, in which we discover that it is not in the chandelier-lit drawing room but below stairs that the keys to the mystery are found.

The third notion, related to both of the above, is the idea of strong objectivity. Articulated in the work of Sandra Harding (1991), and developed by others working in feminist epistemology, this affirms that the best knowledge of the world is developed from those who feel most sharply where the shoe pinches. But this in itself is not enough. What is required is the ability to hear differing perspectives on the same issue, and to respond to these empathetically in order to gain fresh insights into your own position. Harding writes:

[T]o enact or operationalise the directive of strong objectivity is to value the Other's perspective and pass over in thought to the social condition that

---

6   If we think of the wild zone metaphysically, or in terms of consciousness, it has
     no equivalent male space since all of male consciousness is within the circle of the
     dominant structure and thus accessible to or structured by language ... In terms
     of cultural anthropology, women know what the male circle is like, even if they
     have never seen it, because it becomes the subject of legend ... But men do not
     know what is in the wild. (Showalter 1986b: 262)

creates it – not in order to stay there, to 'go native' or merge the self with the Other, but in order to look back on the self with all its cultural particularity from a more distant, critical, objectifying location. (1991: 151)

So what of all this in preaching? Well, partly because of my understanding of accountability, and partly because of my understanding of Christianity (which is, after all, why I am a preacher), I think it is my duty to step down from the pedestal of the universal and speak from the vantage point of my location, my body. I think it is also necessary to break the silence of the muted zone and find language to articulate perspectives that are not usually heard in Church. I similarly attempt to pass over into the realm of the silenced Other and to attempt to try to see my own world from this place.

In the past I have written (1999; 2003) and spoken about my experience of infertility and frequently referred to this in preaching. I found that speaking from personal experience of this muted zone about the mundane grief of the body enabled people with differing, particular, silenced griefs to acknowledge and articulate them. This has confirmed me in the view that preachers do not need to rely upon 'common human experience' to inform their preaching. We should not locate ourselves at the safe place where the personal recedes beyond our vision but rather stand where the particular embraces the particular. This, at least, is the place that I am best able to communicate.

But of course many problems remain. Not least, the vexed question of our ethical responsibilities in relation to those who have no voice, no platform or pulpit.

White feminists, particularly academic feminists, have had to learn that they cannot claim to speak on behalf of all women. In the process we have discovered that there is a comfort in silence. Hélène Cixous raises powerful challenges to those women who for reasons of political correctness decide to remain silent rather than speak 'on behalf' of others. She poses her dilemma as a poet thus:

> Can a poet permit him or herself, and does she have the strength to speak about that which has been reduced to silence. Wouldn't this be blasphemy? Isn't it a necessity? Isn't this exactly what we must do, knowing all the while the paradox? … My choice has been made. After all I have decided to speak about that which takes our breath away. Because more than anything else I am suspicious of silence. (Cixous, in MacGillivray 1994: xlix)

I, too, have decided to speak about what takes the breath away but do so with many unresolved dilemmas concerning my accountability (questions of authority creep back in here!) to those for whom I fabricate a voice. I predict that questions relating to the ethics of advocacy and the status of testimony are likely to be ones that will occupy feminist preachers further in the future as we continue to be confronted with the challenge of speaking out of our relation with those who have been reduced to silence.

A quick decision and a wrong one

I can still remember the lecture. I was listening to it, not giving it, then: 'the three elements of preaching are exegesis (not eisegisis – that is the sin against the Holy Spirit), illustration, application. Application is of the utmost importance. Never let the sermon end without pointing out to the congregation the implications of what they have heard. For the word to live it must be acted upon.' I took this advice to heart and tried to follow it. I spent a number of years telling congregations, made up mainly of elderly people possessing degrees of faith and a wisdom I shall probably never attain, to join revolutionary social movements or, if infirmity and incapacity prevented this, to at least spend every spare moment sending letters to MPs, befriending refugees and opening their doors to the homeless. At the very least they could refuse to sing the horrible sexist words in their hymn books.

Happy days …

I don't do this much any more. I now wrestle with this issue of application. It seems to me that Solomon wants to do what many preachers want to do and that is to make a quick, clear judgement that resolves the situation and removes from himself all the guilt of association. He wishes to make a strong, clean cut rather than tend a weeping wound. When I picture the judgement scene it brings to my mind all the violent horror of innocent faith.

A couple of years ago there was a poll to find the nation's favourite book. One of mine, *The Quiet American* (1955) by Graham Greene, did very well. I think a major factor in its appeal is that it shows how dangerous innocence is. The young idealist of the title sees himself as a soldier of light and believes that he can judge what is best, promote decency, democracy, true love in a situation of the greatest complexity and ambiguity. So bright is his vision that he is prepared to use the most savage means to achieve it. In the context of the current war in Iraq the book has a remarkably contemporary feel. It is not good enough to say that Tony Blair really believed he was doing the right thing. Not good enough at all.

So, if we are not to make Solomon's mistake, there is the need to take a long hard look at ourselves and recognize our own complicity in the issues we are addressing. In my midrash I used the phrase 'mothers do kill their own children' and, I think, one of the reasons I used it was because of the impact that the novel *Beloved* (Morrison 1987) has made upon feminist theology. Kathleen Sands comments upon this very perceptively in her book *Escape from Paradise* (1994), when she argues that *Beloved* represents the deepest possible acknowledgement of humanity's lost innocence (1994: 142). But Sands argues that looking upon horror need not turn us into stone; 'inescapable guilt can be a source of moral information' (1994: 145). Goodness is not something we possess and others lack. Rather we can view it as a fragile construction heroically crafted in the midst of compromising circumstances.

In the times we live in, we are deeply aware of how implicated we are in the evils we condemn. The preacher has work to do communicating this uncomfortable reality, and it may be that we need to give ourselves fully to this before we can see clearly how to act for transformation (an analysis of the ecological crisis and the situation in the Middle East would certainly lend credence to this conviction). However, the fact that I no longer easily append a list of possible applications to each sermon I write does not mean I have lost hope that my preaching has effect, that it might provoke faithful action, bring change. I am making a gamble here. Gambling that something powerful is happening when I preach, through the telling of stories, the creation of symbols and metaphors, poesis.

I am inciting people to imagine. I am trusting imagination is transformative and that poetry creates change. Rowan Williams argues, 'The truth with which the poetic text is concerned is not verification but manifestation. That is to say that the text displays, or even embodies, the reality with which it is concerned simply by witness or "testimony"' (1986: 199). As I discussed previously (see pages 52–4), what I am reaching for are ways of speaking that provoke an encounter or epiphany. I am also seeking words virulent enough to invade our consciousness as an infection, virus, stain or taint. Words that will mutate our minds. Rubem Alves argues that sacred words must be eaten and become your flesh (1990). Let me give an example here.

There is a story that goes something like this:

A man was walking through Glasgow, and he was set upon by youths who knocked him into the gutter and stole his credit cards. As he was lying there along came a city councillor who was on his way to a crime prevention meeting. 'Well that's another statistic for the record,' he said as he passed by. Then along came a preacher who was on his way to deliver a sermon about family values. 'This is what happens when a society neglects to discipline its young,' he said as he passed by.
Finally along came a rough sleeper with a dog on a piece of string. He lifted the man from the gutter. 'Would you like a cup of tea mate?' he said. 'It's not been your lucky day. I'll treat you.'

Here is a different story:

There was a father who had two daughters. He abused them both. They grew to adulthood but were unable to break the chains of control he had bound around them. Then the youngest daughter suffered a breakdown.

She realized that her recovery depended upon confronting her father with what he had done and telling him that she would no longer play his games any more. She allowed him to see her fierce anger and her pain. It was probably not her words, but the resolute way in which she resisted his coercion that made her father realize he was an ageing man who could no longer dominate his child. The power he relied upon was broken. He sought his younger daughter's help. 'What must I do?' he said. 'You must beg forgiveness from my sister,' she said. He agreed to do so. But the elder sister became angry when she realized what had happened. She could not bear her own shame and humiliation being brought to light. She refused to speak to her sister and continued to behave as the obedient child of her father.

Both of the stories I have told could be used by preachers reflecting upon the parable of the Good Samaritan and the parable of the Prodigal Son, respectively. However, it is usually only the first form of retelling (in a variety of similar forms) that is heard in Church. We take a story already familiar and make it even more so. We experience warm feelings of recognition when we hear the tale told in our vernacular tongue. You could say the first story displays more respect for the original because it follows it more closely. However, all the scandal of the story has evaporated. The retelling is conventional and affirms our preconceptions of what the parable means today. The second story is harder to handle. It confuses the hearer. Who is God? The father with his awful abusive power or the younger daughter in her determined resistance? Actually, it is difficult to say. Both figures have divine attributes and the story causes us to think about these differently. Similarly, the new narrative raises very uncomfortable dilemmas. We are happy when the wounded contemporary 'traveller from Jerusalem to Jericho' enjoys a cup of hot, sweet tea with his new friend. We are not comfortable thinking about forgiveness in the context of abuse. Is forgiveness adequate here? Is it more dangerous than healing? What are the bounds of forgiveness and how do we respond to its 'prodigal' challenge? The second story makes us work hard, as the hearers of the original parable would have had to work hard, to reorder our world.

Did not God himself smite down the first child?

While we are contemplating the stories preachers don't tell, I wonder if you can recall this one:

> When the wife of Uriah the Hittite heard that her husband was dead she made lamentation for him. When the mourning was over David sent for her ... and she bore his child. But the Lord struck the child that she bore

to David and it became sick … On the seventh day the child died.

David comforted his wife Bathsheba and went and lay with her and she bore a son called Solomon and the Lord loved him and sent a message to David that he be named Jedidiah. Beloved of God. (2 Sam. 12)

When reflecting upon the story of Solomon's judgement a painful thought came powerfully to my mind. This is an echo story. The king stood erect with his sword held high over the vulnerable body of a child is but a mirror image of a previous judgement. God 'himself' stood as both judge and executioner over Bathsheba's baby – Solomon's brother. In this earlier story, however, the sword falls and the child is murdered: a divine victim.

Women who are wrestling to preach out of the male-centred traditions of the sacred text are brought face to face with a similar discomforting awareness. The stories, apparently safely ordered in our lectionaries (how comforting to know we are in Year B, second Sunday of Epiphany, proceeding safely on our carefully signposted route through the scriptures), are bound up with, and cannot be disassociated from, such scenes of sacrificial violence. At the very heart of the Christian faith lie texts of terror[7] that, through repetition and re-enactment, continue to have a powerful impact.

Marjorie Procter-Smith (1998: 428–33) demonstrates how our routine liturgical practices, which include the recitation of scripture, entail gestures of submission and appeasement towards a potentially violent power. Her concern is the effect that the ritual re-enactments of these sentiments have upon the many women who endure the mundane reality of domestic violence. Similarly, Rita Nakashima Brock (1988) interrogates the way in which the everyday use of the symbolics of atonement works to create a culture in which the abuse and sacrifice of children is subliminally normalized and unofficially condoned.

The question that challenges me continually is: how can I respond to the slaughter of the innocents, which is an irreducible legacy of the Christian tradition? In what ways can I articulate the horror that is inextricably woven with the beauty and the holiness of the faith in which I have been formed? I have come to accept that many women will see no hope of redemption within a tradition that is implicated in so many holocausts. However, others of us dare to visit the scenes of loss and desolation and work to transform the 'texts of terror' into memorials, into places we can approach to mourn, to understand, to bear witness and grow wise.

This is dark and dismal work and yet religious yearnings for a divine encounter that will lift us into another realm, where nothing is hurt or

---

7   A phrase popularized after Phyllis Trible's influential book *Texts of Terror* (1992).

wounded or suffers, are very dangerous indeed. It is for this reason that I have personally come to revalue the experience of working within the difficult confines of an old religion. Whilst I rebuild the walls and tend the altar fires I am acutely aware that the sacred past I guard has been bloody and violent – particularly towards women. However, I find this awareness more creative than the illusion that it is possible to wipe the traces away and begin again to create religious structures that have never tasted the knowledge of good and evil. The challenge that I must perpetually address is how to create a way of mediating what is dangerous and deathly in such ways that its harm will not be perpetuated upon future generations. This requires new rituals, new ways of preaching to be created which can contemplate the horrors we can no longer afford to ignore.

Naming the dead

When I began teaching theology in Manchester in the late 1980s I was fortunate in making contact with a number of women who were experimenting with new forms of preaching. We were tackling issues relating to women's experience that we felt had been long neglected and we were seeking to exploit the positive vantage point of a female body in articulating sacred truths. Although we were at different stages of life, and some were single and others childless, we found that many of these early sermons returned again and again to a particular theme: the death or loss of babies.

At that time the fact that a number of us should be meditating on this uncommon topic seemed to me to represent our determination to resignify what the Christian tradition had resolutely repressed. We were zealous that the human cost of divine creativity should be spoken of in the sanctuary in the context of continued faithful commitment. We were determined to pursue the deconstructive power of the question, 'What has been lost?' to its limits.

Now re-reading the collection of sermons that emerged from our joint work (Walton and Durber 1994) I am struck by how much emotional distress is being articulated through our defiant words. I find that the sermons are giving voice to a collective pain which comes from the knowledge that so much which pertains to women in our religious tradition has been allowed to perish unnamed and without memorials. More than this I can also hear the echoes of personal grief in our re-telling of the ancient stories. Through our preaching we were making space to mourn what in ourselves had been wasted, lost or unable to thrive because of the roles we had felt compelled to assume in our spiritual and professional lives.

In the legends surrounding Solomon, the pain of his birth and the tragedy of Bathsheba's lost baby unsettle the triumphalist narrative. In the story, which is supposed to confirm his legendary powers, a still and lifeless child lies neglected and abandoned – a reminder of this unspoken past. It is my hope that through accomplishing the proper rites of naming and mourning, feminist preachers might attend to the birth of a new wisdom. I hope that we shall at last be able to claim that what past traditions and present practice have ignored in the experience of women can be named beloved of God.

Wisdom's children

In many of the legends surrounding the meeting of Solomon and the Queen of Sheba there is the suggestion that the 'delight'[8] he gave her issued in the birth of a child. In my midrash I have used this ancient belief to signify my own commitment to the future of preaching – and consequently to the life of the Church. Like many feminists I desire the tradition that I contest with and engage in the deepest and most intimate relations with it. I take the risk of conceiving within myself out of its generative force.

But look at what I have conceived. My reflections upon preaching have been structured around a midrash that deliberately disputes the terms of the first narrative. It is a 'made up' story that sits in an uneasy relationship with what remains the 'authoritative' (that word again) text. This might not be so much of a problem if the context were a seminar room, or a creative writing group. But my preaching from the pulpit draws upon all the narrative devices I have used here. I consciously preach through fiction, while many would argue that preaching should be all about truth telling. It would require another essay to reflect fully upon the implications of this strategy. For now, I could simply state that for women speaking from the place where they have been silenced there are few other options open to them. Or I might recall that twentieth-century theology from Barth to Bultmann has been fascinated by the transformative space between the text and the Word – and so am I! Whenever the sacrament of preaching takes place some form of transubstantiation is involved.

The closing passage of my midrash contains a thread that binds it back again to the living body of my tradition. It offers the trace of a Christology. It is only a trace, but it nevertheless refers onwards to an image that has helped to sustain many Christian feminists who find themselves alienated from the dominant symbols of the Christian faith.[9] The vision of Jesus as the child of wisdom[10] helps us to recover a maternal genealogy in the religion of the Father and the Son. Through meditating upon it we can

---

8   1 Kgs 10.13.
9   See, for example, Fiorenza (1995).
10   'Wisdom is justified by all her children', Lk. 7.35.

remember Mary and Sheba and all the other mothers of wisdom. We can also claim our own power to participate in the work of divine incarnation.

This birthing of the Word is the preacher's task.

Chapter 6

Are the Words Really Lost? Feminist Revisionist Myth Making in the Work of Michèle Roberts

Re-vision – the act of looking back, of seeing with fresh eyes, of entering an old text from a new critical direction – is for women more than a chapter in cultural history: it is an act of survival. (Rich 1978b: 35)

In her famous essay 'When We Dead Awaken: Writing as Re-vision' (1978b), the poet Adrienne Rich passionately articulates her conviction that women seeking a transformed future must not turn their backs upon the past. She argues that the weight of history cannot be 'shrugged off' but the burden it imposes upon women might be transformed into a strange blessing. In particular sacred traditions expressed through mythology, literature and art can be revisioned. Although the narratives that sustain culture are dangerous for women they also carry within them evidence of an unclaimed inheritance. Through attentive re-readings women may begin to claim their own erased genealogy. This will entail a painstaking effort of creative interpretation:

> To do this work takes a capacity for constant active presence, a naturalist's attention to minute phenomena, for reading between the lines, watching closely for symbolic arrangements, decoding difficult and complex messages left for us by women of the past. (1978b: 13)

Rich's essay represents a significant moment in the development of contemporary feminism. Women working in many cultural spheres sought to critique the male-centred traditions through which they had been formed and also to engage with them in order that they might be reclaimed and transformed.[1] The work of the pioneering feminist biblical scholar Elizabeth Schussler Fiorenza (1983) can be seen as paradigmatic of this painstaking revisioning labour. She interrogated biblical texts used to subjugate women but also lovingly examined these same scriptures for traces of the female past. Because the evidence of women's participation in the formation of culture must be assembled from fragments, gaps and silences, Fiorenza soon came to realize that her work was creative as well as exegetical. The past is not only remembered; it is recreated. This task requires imaginative as well as interpretative resources.

Within the literary sphere feminist revisionists followed similar routes. They critiqued the way male authors employed myths and also sought to rediscover the spiritual wisdom of women which could then be used as a symbolic resource by women writers. This 'women's tradition' had to be both remembered and imagined and the development of revisionist mythology within women's creative writing came to be seen as a political move to address the history of women's cultural exclusion and transform the spiritual archives of Western culture.

My concern in this chapter is to explore this literary revisioning work as it is displayed in the work of one particular writer, Michèle Roberts. Roberts is an author whose literary journey has tracked the parallel trajectory of the women's movement and whose work displays a lively awareness of contemporary literary theory. As such it offers a privileged window into how a deeply engaged woman writer views the potential of revisioning a generation after Rich called upon women artists to awake the dead.

Wild girl

Roberts is the daughter of a French Catholic mother and an English Protestant father. Much of her writing focuses upon living between worlds, speaking different tongues and being both a stranger and insider to traditions. She was educated into Catholicism but, perhaps due to her mother's practical and earthly spirituality, she came to see her religion as 'integral as the blood in my veins, passed onto me by my mother like milk (1983: 52). She also intuitively grasped that within it moved many shadows. Catholic feasts overlaid the older pagan celebrations and rituals around birth, sexuality and death (1983: 53). Roberts' childhood years were infused with a sense of communion with the God who

---

[1]   This development within 'second wave feminism' was preceded by the engagement of women writers throughout the twentieth century with archetypal cultural symbols and ancient myths. See M. Humm (1994: 54–73).

animated all things but within this also lurked a sense of yearning for deeper connection to the maternal divine, a 'queenly Virgin Mary the land flowing with milk and honey, and I was the Israelites in exile yearning to be united with her' (1983: 54).

Encounters with Marxism and feminism led Roberts to embrace political activism and to repudiate her childhood faith. She sought to 'excize memory and the past, my unconscious and the system of images which had formed me' (1983: 58). This process of excision was too radical and realizing that she was in danger of self-mutilation Roberts entered psychotherapy. The Jungian archetypes she encountered enabled her to construct positive images of female identity and thus survive depression. She claimed for herself the archetypal image of the Sybil:

> the creative woman who is in touch with ancient memories, inspiration, who is an artist. This system of imagery helped me to see that sexuality and spirituality can be connected, need not be at war. Also that a woman can be complete in herself, not a companion or a shadow to a man, but a distinct being, different to him, in her own right. (1983: 62)

A new confidence in her spiritual identity was expressed in a revisionist novel that affirms the desiring relations between masculine and feminine archetypes and the love relation that can exist between a free creative woman and ancient religious traditions. In *The Wild Girl, The Book of the Testimony of Mary Magdalene* (1991 [1984]) Roberts employs Jungian archetypes but also draws upon historical traditions marginalized within the Christian West which feminist scholars (e.g. Elaine Pagels 1988; Rosemary Ruether 1983 and Asphodel Long 1992) have argued contain the traces of submerged female traditions. Roberts is particularly indebted to her eclectic study of the Nag Hammadi documents and Gnostic Christian texts. Out of these she creates many images of the reconciliation of the new Adam and the new Eve. She employs her Mary to carry a secret message entrusted to her by Jesus:

> The separation of the inner man and the inner woman is a sickness, a great wound. I Christ came to repair the separation and to reunite the two and restore to life and health those in danger of dying of this sickness of the soul … What is this rebirth? How is it to be achieved? The image of this rebirth is a marriage. (1991: 110)

The sexual love between Jesus and Mary is the lens through which Roberts views the misogyny and violence of her inherited tradition. By making her characters lovers Roberts touches the place of pain women experience in relation to the eradication of female sexuality from the dominant tradition. Through presenting women's sexual knowledge as a form of spiritual wisdom Roberts challenges the ancient dualisms that have circumscribed women's power. In the process she re-visions divine and human authority and presents male and female existence as potentially harmonious; capable of generating interpenetrating erotic pleasure rather than perpetual enmity. In the dispensation of the new Adam and the new Eve both genders are embodied, spiritual and sacred.

Fire and ash

The hopefulness which animates *The Wild Girl* does not disappear from Roberts' later writing but in many of the novels and poetry which follow we are presented with much darker pictures of the quest women must undergo in order to discover again their spiritual inheritance. This is evident if we compare *The Wild Girl* with one of Roberts' most powerful later novels, *Daughters of the House* (1992). In the first the narrator presents herself as a witness to truth and commends her story confidently to those who will receive it and pass it on to others. In contrast *Daughters of the House* is about the failure to remember and its consequences. It is about the violence at the root of faith and the hatred of maternal power in monotheistic traditions. It is about death and in particular the death of the mother. The opening words of this novel are far removed from the statements of confidence and faith that introduce *The Wild Girl*:

> Antoinette laughed. She was buried in the cellar under a heap of sand. Her mouth was stuffed full of torn-up letters and broken glass but she was tunnelling her way out like a mole. Her mouth bled from the corners. She laughed a guttural laugh, a Nazi laugh ...
>
> Antoinette was dead, which was why they had buried her in the cellar. She moved under the heap of sand. She clutched her red handbag which was full of the shreds of dead flesh. She was trying to get out, to hang two red petticoats on the washing-line in the orchard. Sooner or later she would batter down the cellar door and burst up through it on her dead and bleeding feet. (1992: 1)

This novel, set in rural France during and after the Second World War, tells the story of two cousin/sisters, Léonie and Thérèse, whose mother Antoinette lies dead, beyond speech, her mouth stuffed with torn-up letters, the corners bleeding. But although buried this mother reaches out towards her daughters. Antoinette, the mother, is symbolically linked with a powerful female divine presence. The story tells how this archaic female power was worshipped in the past. The village community had venerated an ancient stone image in a sacred grove. Acts of communal devotion to 'the lady' had marked the passage between fertility and death for generations. Respect for a power beyond 'the name of the Father' had given coherence to the community and enabled it to mediate the destructive and regenerative energy of close social relations. When this form is destroyed by the local priest the village falls prey to the fascistic brutality of the times – a violent force that seeks to destroy all that threatens paternal order.

Sensing the significance of the broken fragments of the lady, Antoinette hides the pieces in the cellar of the family home. To conceal and protect this hidden power she is compelled to engage in collaborative intercourse with the German soldiers occupying the village. Her future is sealed by this act and Antoinette never fully recovers from her wartime experience. Her early death blights the childhood of both girls.

Thérese copes with Antoinette's death by finding herself another mother, 'she'd been sold one ready made by the priests of her church. Perfect, that Mother of God, that pure Virgin, a holy doll who never felt angry or sexy and never went away. The convent was the only place that she could preserve that image intact' (1992: 165). She joins a religious order and seeks to assuage her grief through piety and ritual. The holy virgin is venerated as a substitute for her lost mother and the female divine. For many years Thérese clings to this image but the substitute fails to satisfy her and a restless longing drives her to return to her village and her maternal home. She is seeking her real mother and hoping to provoke Léonie to explore the buried memories of the past.

Léonie does not welcome this return. She has become a village matriarch who actively sustains the family home and the institutions of the local community. Her life is dedicated to obliterating the chaos of origins and preventing the horrors of the past from impacting upon domestic routines and social relations. However, not only does the lady of red fire still lie broken in pieces and buried in the cellar, there are other alien and disruptive presences that have been hidden within the house – a shrine Léonie tends with beeswax and fresh linen. Jewish prisoners had been secreted there prior to their clandestine execution by Nazi sympathizers. But the dead are not quiet.

Léonie must, at last, acknowledge the claims they make upon her. She confronts her mother's death, the tangled roots of her own identity, and opens herself to the confused images and sensations she has repressed. In this new state of awareness she also remembers the war crimes committed in her small village. Empowered by her consciousness of loss Léonie is able to confront what she has expelled from memory. She becomes an agent of change, and possible redemption, rather than a keeper of the house. The novel ends as Léonie opens the door to a room she had previously kept closed. It was a room that as children the sisters had been discouraged from entering 'in case they'd heard those voices crying out and were frightened by them ... But history was voices that came alive and shouted' (1992: 171).

In this later work re-visioning is offered to us as a process of becoming aware of dead voices that come alive and shout. Gone are the images of tender desire. This is a desperately painful process as it entails contemplating the violence that has orphaned the daughters and which maintains a culture of hostility towards the stranger. The novel, however, has a positive and redemptive conclusion. This is more difficult to discern in a later novel that confronts the Christian past.

Ghost writing

Although *Impossible Saints* (1998) is a very funny novel there is a sense of irrecoverable loss running through it that is more disquieting than that found in *Daughters of the House*. The work, partly inspired by the life of St Teresa of Avila, loosely narrates the story of 'Josephine' – interspersed with other stories echoing the lives of Christian women saints. The story begins as Josephine discovers the clandestine pleasures of reading enjoyed by her mother Beatrice and her woman friends:

> Books were their drugs, the magic carpets onto which they flung themselves in order to be borne somewhere else, books lifted them up like powerful caressing hands and cradled them like mothers do, as though they were babies to be held and fed … All the books became one book, they streamed into each other, a channel of sparkling water which kept all the garden green, in the midst of the encircling desert, and never ran dry. (1998: 43).

After her mother's death Josephine discovers that the chest of books her mother has always carefully locked contains not only romances but also books on herbs and medicine, anatomy, dangerous knowledge. It also contains mysterious scrolls wrapped in golden cloth. Josephine and her cousin Magdalena eagerly begin to read these forbidden texts but their transgression (and the 'wanton' behaviour it encourages) are discovered by Josephine's father:

> Magdalena was bundled away, and Josephine forbidden ever to see her again. Ferdinand burned all of Beatrice's books that he could find, and the chest that had held them. He made Josephine feed the fire, handing the books to her one at a time. They took a long time to burn. Solid blocks of words, blackening, black, transformed into packets of feathery ash that finally fell apart. (1998: 51)

Josephine is sent to a convent from which she does not emerge for many years. She finds sweet comfort there in erotic visions of Christ but this is a time of burning when visionaries and heretics are raised on pyres; 'The

world was red' (1998: 136). Josephine must protect herself by writing her
life in orthodox and conventional tones for the Inspectors.[2] But the writing
is false. It is constructed out of fear and lying. Her confessor (and lover)
advises her that she must begin writing herself again. To do so entails
leaving the convent and entering Magdalena's house. This is a place of
earthly delights where her mother's golden scrolls (rescued by Magdalena)
are hidden. These scrolls are Gnostic texts and reading them Josephine is
enraptured. She is drawn into an untranslatable archaic language:

> Josephine [was] now a part of its grammar, earth sentences, the earth was
> the speech she could hear, that spoke her and spoke to her, that attracted
> her into its structure and dissolved her into a part of a speech, a part of
> earth ... She and the earth were the same body. (1998: 190)

Her readings convince Josephine that another form of spiritual life is
possible for women that does not entail a renunciation of their sexuality
or bodily wisdom but allows them periodically to withdraw from the
world to nurture their creative spirits. Such a utopian vision is, of course,
unachievable in the time of the Inspectors and Josephine dies leaving only
a legacy of writing; her secret life. Small fragments in shrunken
handwriting, disordered pages, 'a chaotic pattern which made no sense'
(1998: 238). Even these fragile scattered writings, 'discarded all over the
house like vegetable peelings in a bin or balls of fluff under a cupboard'
(1998: 235) are lost or stolen by the guardians of religion. There is
nothing left. Her niece Isabel seeking to remember her aunt is haunted by
the echoes of disjointed phrases and in the end, rather than accept the
silence, allows her aunt to invade her imagination. In the warm space of
recollection she 'invents' her. 'I reassemble her from jigsaw bits and
pieces of writing; from scattered parts. I make her up. She rises anew in
my words' (1998: 290).

The story of Josephine is a story of women and writing. She is forbidden
to read, her books are burned, her words are lost; really lost. It is also a
narrative of re-visioning; of the impossibility of restoring the past and the
limits of remembering. The accounts of other Christian women saints
whose stories are told alongside Josephine's emphasize the utter annihi-
lation of women's words and voices. Clever, funny and creative female
saints come to life on the pages only to be obliterated. They die 'in the
ice of the cave, frozen solid inside it' (1998: 95). They perish at 'the bottom
of the well ... flesh and bones rotted and disintegrated and [become] part
of the filthy water (1998: 174). They are 'shrivelled up like an old root
buried under moss and branches' (1998: 209). Josephine herself is

---

[2]   The narrative here reflects feminist conjectures concerning the written legacy of
St Teresa.

dismembered limb from limb. Her bones lost amongst the mixed bones from 11,000 virgins (1998: 307). In this later work we are confronted with the bleak awareness that the revisionist writer is calling up shadows and spectres from the past. She is unable to breathe life into dry bones.

Possibly she's absurd

This chapter has explored the work of Michèle Roberts as an example of a woman writer engaged in the feminist literary revisioning of theological traditions. In her work I identify an approach to the religious past which is sensitive to the history of violence and exclusion it represents for women. We can also discern the conviction that women have created their own spiritual traditions and have actively resisted when these were silenced or forbidden. Her writing bears testimony to the fact that women writers continue to contest male religious authority and create their own divine symbolic landscape through remembering and imagining.

To read Roberts as representative of a feminist revisioning is also to admit that some of the common criticisms that are made of this form of literary intervention can be applied with justification to her work. Significant amongst these is the charge that they are following paths established by male exegetes, male 'romantics', psychoanalysts and literary critics. There is nothing inherently feminist in revisioning *per se* and the effect of offering multiple re-readings of a sacred tradition is to strengthen that tradition rather than to challenge it. It has also been argued that the notion that religious myths are the vehicles through which archetypal symbols form culture and the psyche is itself a deeply conservative notion that reflects the critical environment of the 1950s and 60s and is unsustainable today (see Humm 1994: 55). Roberts might also be accused of offering readers images of female spirituality that are erotic, fleshly, earth related and ecstatic – as opposed to the rational, ethical and transcendent sacred traditions of men. Through so doing she may be perpetuating binary and hierarchical understandings of masculine and feminine spheres rather than radically challenging our understandings of gendered identity. It must be admitted that the sacred traditions of Western culture offer a very limited set of roles for women and some religious feminists have preferred to look to the future rather than the past when constructing imaginative projections of female power (see Christ 1979: 230).

These points are worthy of serious attention. But although engaging with male-centred religious traditions is precarious work for the woman artist I believe Roberts is well aware of the ambivalence of the task she is undertaking. Alongside erotic imagery Roberts offers darker images of the revisioning process. The feminist revisionist writer opens herself up not only to receive the body of her lover and generate new life. She also allows the dead to inhabit her body. The medium cannot herself raise the dead and in bringing the past to view she risks becoming a vehicle for a return of archaic male power as well as female wisdom. But the sacred past calls to the woman artist and she responds.

Roberts' ironic, self-reflexive poem 'Restoration Work in Palazzo Te' (1995) describes the compulsion to attend to this inheritance but acknowledges that the effort may be misguided. In this work a young female mural restorer becomes Psyche searching out Eros. With her diagrams and photographic images she returns to her 'house of desire' to 'revision it' (1995: 57). But the forms are breaking up, the original paint flakes from the walls and is lost. Despite this she continues her work attending to what has almost vanished. Eros resents this attention and stubbornly resists the restoring touch of her hands. Covered in white dust, aware that the task may be impossible and her faith absurd, she nevertheless continues to attend with painstaking effort to 'the work that matters' (1995: 57).

Chapter 7

Extreme Faith in the Work of Elizabeth Smart and Luce Irigaray

A book about love

In the late November of 1939, aspiring author Elizabeth Smart wrote in her journal: 'I want my book to be about love. But love is so large and formless (But so full of new worlds)' (1992a: 231). Given the political circumstances at the time of this entry, Smart's words could easily be read as confirming the stereotypical view of the woman author as particularly afflicted by romantic myopia. As the world descends into chaos Smart perversely chooses to expend her creative energies on the emotional and particular, the ahistorical and the apolitical. She might thus be accused of nurturing an immoral escapism in the face of impending disaster. This was certainly the view of Smart's own mother Louie, a popular Canadian society hostess, who had lately turned to knitting scarves and serving tea to soldiers. 'Do you consider your writing is a sufficient contribution to a troubled and war-torn world?' she wrote in a disapproving letter to her daughter (Sullivan 1992: 151–2).

In this chapter I shall explore more deeply Smart's wartime endeavours to write a book about love. To do so I shall draw upon her journals, poetry and the 'prose work'[1] for which she is best known, *By Grand Central Station I Sat Down and Wept* (1992a [1945]). My hope here is to make manifest the scandalous vision that inspired Smart's wartime writing in order to assess its significance for today. My interrogation of Smart's work is intended to raise questions concerning the engagement of contem-

---

[1]   Smart referred to her two short literary texts as prose works to stress their distinction from works conforming to conventional novelistic or poetic genres.

porary feminist theory with Western culture, a culture engaged in what Hélène Cixous has described as a war against women and other living creatures (Cixous 1982) and to provoke theological reflection upon these themes. I begin by focusing upon Smart's own understanding of her creative project.

Another instrument to play on

Smart's journal entries in the closing days of 1939 record a massive change in self-perception and signal the birth of a confidence that she was at last able to create work which was distinctive, powerful and, in her opinion, of vital significance in the context of the times. This assurance had been achieved as a result of a complete reversal in the opinions she had formerly held concerning the work of writing – a vocation which had obsessed her since childhood.

As a young woman, moving in the most fashionable cultural circles of her native Canada, Smart had met, and eagerly interrogated, a number of successful writers. From these juvenile encounters she had fashioned an understanding of writing as an exalted occupation whose practice was far removed from the 'trivial' concerns of material life (and particularly the life of the body). She had to come to regard literature as a spiritual pursuit requiring the highest degree of self-discipline, dedication and detachment. The sacred task of the writer was to convey the highest truths in the purest forms. She understood poetry, in particular, as an attempt to form an image of the Word in words. However, despite these intellectual convictions she was unable to achieve the detached vantage point she coveted. She was possessed of that uncertain sense of self which appears to be the experience of many poets and visionaries (she cherished the writing of the English mystics and enjoyed the verse of William Blake). The barrier separating her identity from the rest of the living world was felt as fragile and permeable. Furthermore, her strong desires continually drew her away from the austere work to which she felt herself called. An early journal entry expresses the tensions she experienced. As she contemplates dedicating herself to poetry she feels 'the round softness' of her breasts and is overcome by the sense that her physical being and erotic desires are calling her away from words of 'eternal rightness' to the immediacy of an embrace. Perhaps it is only men who can resolve this dichotomy? Smart fears she may lack the strength to pursue her spiritual vocation. The breast that falls 'voluptuously' into her hand reminds her that she is not a poet but a woman (1992b: 70).

In order to fulfil the poet's calling Smart strove to arm herself with appropriate weapons to fight 'the irresistible, the compelling monster sex' (1992b: 62). She lost the battle. However, through her unheroic capitulation, and particularly as a result of her passionate sexual relationships with the artist Jean Varda and poet Alice Paalen, she began to view her writer's body, her woman's body, as an invaluable resource rather than an enemy to be subdued: 'But it is another instrument I want to play upon. My rich brain had abundant words, gorged while my body waited. Waited anguished, but now – those rich folds fall between the page and me and I say what is a poem?' (1992b: 252). Poetry, the nature and the purpose of writing all needed to be rethought, as did the problem of constructing a style of expression that was reflective of her sexed body. The distinction Smart had formerly held between the spiritual world to which the writer aspires and the intoxicating world of the flesh had fallen away. 'It is God. It is sex', (1992b: 182) she could affirm, and no longer sought to convey in her writing concepts 'less inextricably woven with the undiluted flesh' (1992b: 280). Her task was now rather to develop a form of writing through which her new understanding of the relation of the body to spirituality might be expressed: 'Entering daily and nightly into the body of God, yet unable to do other than suggest. And now upwards to that staggering vision. Will I have the courage to raise my eyes? Can I face the things I laboriously flee?' (1992b: 187).

Cradle the seed

Viewed through the lens of Smart's sensual mysticism her intention to write a book about love appears in a rather different light. It is by no means uncommon for male and female writers to celebrate a sense of communion with the natural world. It is not unusual for male writers – we might think of D. H. Lawrence, Miller, Bataille – to express a mystical appreciation of (phallic) sexuality. However, as Irigaray has argued, the woman who speaks as active lover rather than passive beloved, who speaks from appreciation of the erotic potential of the female body, is a figure largely absent from representation in Western culture.[2] What I have termed Smart's sensual mysticism still remains an unusual authorial perspective in women's writing. However, this does not mean that her work can avoid the charges of romantic escapism mentioned earlier.

To address this issue I return to Smart's own reflections about the significance of her erotic vision, particularly as she struggles to give shape and form to this in her journal entries for the significant period towards the end of 1939. Of particular interest is her entry for 5 December in which Smart presents a new statement of her own faith and its implications for her vocation as a writer.

The entry is written in the form of a vision received as she rests under a 'feathery leafed tree' and begins to 'mingle' and become again 'a contin-

---

[2]   Lacanian poststructuralist theory is elaborated around the silence of women's jouissance in the symbolic order.

uation of the earth I walk upon' (1992b: 214). In this state of union and harmony she reflects upon her lover (in this case Jean Varda) and his frantic anxiety and sorrow at the contemporary evils of the world. In the face of this despair Smart defiantly articulates her own unreasonable/immoral faith in a jouissance that overcomes even the profoundest sorrow:

> But I insist on looking the other way like the last pregnant woman in a desolated world. It is a vital thing to keep your eyes on the sun ... to hang on to that hope, to cherish with every ounce of love to be squeezed from the universe, the seed, the frail seed. (1992b: 215)

If she were to lose faith, fail to maintain her vision, then all is lost; 'we shall both be submerged', she writes. There then follows a series of apocalyptic visions supplemented by a rhythmic, rocking litany:

> destruction, desolation, persecution, the terrible final capture, the mountain bursting into flame, all the green grass trampled into cement ... It spreads, it spreads, who can escape?
>   Cradle the seed, cradle the seed, even in the volcano's mouth. (1992b: 215)

I have thought it important to discuss Smart's sensual mysticism,[3] and to show how this vision had begun to shape Smart's response to the conflict which had begun to engulf her world *before* turning to *By Grand Central Station I Sat Down and Wept*. This is because I believe this dimension of the text has been neglected in the past and thus the prose work has not yet received the serious critical attention it deserves.

Smart was a very beautiful woman and she has suffered from being cast as the 'dumb blonde' of the literary world. Her work is frequently described as a remarkable but culturally unmediated account of passion. It is constructed as a 'single sustained climax', we read on the back cover of the recent Flamingo edition. Like Lacan's St Teresa she is held to be experiencing that which she cannot explain. So frustrated was Smart herself by this form of critical sidelining that she produced an annotated companion to her work noting the intertextual references to mythology, philosophy, mystical writing and the poetic tradition it contained. However, this effort did not succeed in shifting the critical consensus that her book is a simple narrative of a personal passion, 'one of the most moving and immediate accounts of a love affair ever written', declares the publisher's preface in my copy of the text (1992a [1945]).

---

[3]   A form of spiritual awareness that comes very close to Irigaray's celebration of the 'sensible transcendental', a God not alien to the female flesh.

Feminist critics have frequently complained that women's writing is assumed to be thinly veiled autobiography rather than a sophisticated literary construction. This book, in particular, is straightforwardly assumed to be the chronicle of Smart's celebrated affair with the poet George Barker which began in July 1940, several months after the extracts I have quoted from her journal were written.[4] I would not wish to deny that this relationship (with Barker) was of great significance for Smart, or that it provided a highly significant experiential resource which Smart draws upon to write her book of love. However, it is a striking fact that *By Grand Central Station* is structured in *an exactly parallel form* to the journal entry for 5 December 1939 in which Smart first presents her testimony of faith and her writing manifesto.

Love as strong as death

Like the journal-vision, the first sections of the prose work contain many images of the female lover mingling with the material world. For example, Smart writes 'I have become part of the earth: I am one of its waves flooding and leaping. I am the same tune now as trees, hummingbirds, fruit, vegetables in rows' (1992a [1945]: 42). These words are in fact adapted from the journal entry with hardly any revision. Or, again, 'the new moss caressed me and the water over my feet and the ferns approved me with endearments: my darling, my darling, lie down with us now for you are earth whom nothing but love can sow' (1992a [1945]: 24).

Smart eschews the naïveté that has marked much feminist theological writing on the relation between women and the nurturing earth. Although sublime, this natural union is not innocent or benign. The creative forces of nature and desire are bloody and murderous as well as fruitful. The God the narrator knows through her body is generative but terrible, 'it is not to be eased from my pain that I crave when I pray to God to understand my corrupt language and step down for a moment to sit on my broken bench. Will there be birth from all this blood?' (1992a [1945]: 32).

The passion the prose work reflects upon is adulterous and guilty: 'On her mangledness I am spreading my amorous sheets' (1992a [1945]: 32). It is costly and all consuming but, the narrator asserts, it focuses tremendous power. Radiant and transforming power. Impossible power. It is compelling to read but difficult to forgive such lines as these:

> There are not too many bereaved or wounded but I can comfort them, and those 5,000,000 who never stop dragging their feet and bundles and

---

[4]   In fact, George Barker did write an agonizing and unsuccessful autobiographical account of the passion. In his story, a dedicated and celebrated poet is lured away from work and wife through the fleshly charms of a female temptress. See Sullivan (1992: 252).

babies with bloated bellies across Europe are not too many, or too benighted, for me to say, Here's a world of hope. I can spare a whole world for each and every one. Set me as a seal upon thine heart … For love is as strong as death. (1992a [1945]: 43-44)

The narrator must be put on trial for such an extreme faith and this is exactly what happens in the next section of the text. In her journal-vision Smart had staked her faith in love in opposition to the forces that deny its sacred power. In the prose work these powers are vividly symbolized. First they appear as the Arizona State Police who arrest the adulterous couple on charges of immorality. Smart composes a powerful intertextual dialogue between the obscene questions of the interrogating officer and the lyrics of the Song of Songs:

Did you sleep in the same room? (Behold thou art fair, my love, behold thou art fair: thou hast dove's eyes.)
In the same bed? (Behold thou art pleasant, also our bed is green.)
Did intercourse take place? (I sat down under his shadow with great delight …) (1992a [1945]: 47)

Next the opposing forces appear in the form of the narrator's father who sits in judgement on his daughter 'with his desk massively symbolic between us' (1992a [1945]: 61). It is not love that matters, he decrees, but duty, decency and proportion. And, finally, the narrator's accuser appears in the most threatening form as the beloved himself.

In her journal-vision Smart's lover was turning away from desire engulfed by pity. So too in the prose work the lovers become estranged because of the man's pity and shame. His feelings for his wife, his guilt about the war and his despair for the world separate him from the narrator. He accuses her. She doesn't care about the world. She is shamefully pregnant when she should share in the barren wastage of the times. These simple lines convey the conflicting worlds that Smart places in symbolic tension: 'You don't take much interest in politics do you? You never read the newspapers? I drank my coffee. I had a slight feeling of nausea. It's to be expected' (1992a [1945]: 76). Confronting this lack of faith as a deadly challenge, the narrator declares herself to be the bearer of healing hope. She makes her personal defence, formally – as if before a judge:

So I say now for the record of myself … I saw that there was nothing else anywhere but this one thing; that neither nunneries, nor Pacific Islands, nor jungles, nor all the Jazz of America, nor the frenzy of warzones could hide any corner which housed an ounce of consolation if this failed. In all states of being in all worlds this is all there is … I do not accept it sadly or ruefully … and though it comes without anything it gives me everything.

With it I can repopulate the world. I can bring forth new worlds in underground shelters while the bombs are dropping: I can do it in lifeboats as the ship goes down. I can do it in prisons without the guards' permission; and oh, when I do it in the lobby while the conference is going on, a lot of statesmen will emerge and see the birth blood and know they have been foiled.

Love is as strong as death. (1992a [1945]: 66)

As well as having the character of testimony this speech is also a testament, final statement, last message. After it is uttered there is nothing left to say. This is the point at which *By Grand Central Station* becomes a tragic tale. The narrator, the last pregnant woman carrying the fragile seeds of hope, cannot reach her beloved: 'He cries out in his sleep. He sees the huge bird of catastrophe fly by. Both its wings are lined with newspaper, five million other voices are shrieking too. How shall I be heard?' (1992a [1945]: 111).

Defeated she lays aside her weapons of love and glimpses the terrible apocalypse. The stage is cleared. As if cleaning an operating theatre after a bloody operation, the station porters wipe the huge floors of Grand Central Station. With their mops and disinfectants they wash away the stains of the 'wailing and bleeding past'. The child that is born from love's betrayal is not the bright bringer of promise but an idiot boy: 'He is America and better than love.' This is the whimpering end of civilisation: 'I myself prefer Boulder Dam to Chartres Cathedral. I prefer dogs to children. I prefer corncobs to the genitals of the male. Everything is hotsy-totsy, dandy, everything's OK' (1992a [1945]: 112).

The body of the woman lover

I have argued that Smart's 'book about love' is not a simple love story, 'the moving and immediate account of a love affair' as we have been told. It is rather a very sophisticated attempt to express a faith which has a completely different foundation to the ethical/political/spiritual systems which Smart has struggled against in relation to her understanding of the work of writing and now engages with in relation to the political crisis of her times. These same systems are the ones which have brought the world to war and the 'pity' (misplaced faith in a disembodied ideal) which they evoke sustains rather than alleviates the violence.

The desiring, passionate, fertile body of the woman lover is placed in symbolic opposition to these forces. It seduces with an entirely other vision. That of an ambivalent, pricey, painful, bloody love which does not need everything imperfect to be swept away, everything chaotic to be ordered and everything tainted to be made clean before generation can occur. It is endlessly prolific. It offers everything in its embrace. Although 'Hope and Europe' lie dying she holds on to love that conceives another, yet unwritten, history and is 'even now big with child' (1992c: 26).

In this frame Smart would be unjustly accused of being uninterested in the war. A pacifist cannot be accused of being disinterested in violence because they refuse to fight. Her intention is to project a radically alternative vision in the midst of the conflict and it is the difference between the two symbolic universes (pity/love) which causes such scandal. It is difficult to tolerate her fecund optimism when we contemplate the devastation out of which her vision is formed. What is particularly challenging is that Smart is fully aware of the extremity of her own faith, 'love is as strong as death', and as heroic as a Christian martyr for her helpless cause.

As I reflect upon the attraction and offence I still feel when I read her work, I remember that Smart was not alone amongst women writers working through the war who set up an alternative female symbolic as a vantage point from which to view the conflict. The poet H. D. celebrates the mystical return of 'the lady' to the blitzed streets of London (H. D. 1983) and Virginia Woolf's fragmentary work *Between the Acts* (1983) ends with the hope of a fecund moment which is passionate and bloody 'in the fields of night'. These women were well known for their radical vision and innovative writing styles. They also found the female body to be a possible alternative location from which to contemplate the conflict and imagine a future very different from the bloody regeneration of masculinist values assumed to take place after the slaughter of the sons.

It is also the case that this writing strategy, placing the body of the woman in the text, is precisely the main achievement of feminist poststructuralism – which currently generates the 'authorized' discourse of academic feminists. Patricia Yaeger, in her classic text *Honey-Mad Women* (1988), welcomes the subversive potential of poststructuralist writing but argues that in order for women to identify with this thinking and claim it as our own 'we must be permitted to see its features in the writing of the past' (1988: 16). Feminist theorists can be accused of 'omitting the practices of real historical women' from their celebration of the utopian potential to be discerned in writing the body. They have remained 'blind to what has actually happened in women's texts' (1988: 20). Following Yaeger I would argue that we can discern a good deal of congruity between Smart's wartime writing and the contemporary symbolics of feminist poststructuralist theory.

There are many parallels to Smart's sensual mysticism in the work of Hélène Cixous on female jouissance and women's writing (see Cixous 1990). The same themes can be observed in Kristeva's early writing on the semiotic (see Kristeva 1980), the maternal realm which has the power to erupt into the cultural order in poetry, mysticism, carnival and revolutionary change. But the parallels are most striking between Smart's work and that of Luce Irigaray. As Irigaray has become the 'feminist philosopher of choice' for many Western feminist academics, it is important to ask what values we are assenting to when we routinely employ her female bodily symbolics in our writings. In what ways does Irigaray's vision represent a politically significant counterforce in the war against women and other living things?

Certainly, Irigaray's faith is no less extreme than Smart's. Whilst her calls for greater cultural attention to be paid to women's bodily experience and maternal genealogies[5] can be seen as straightforwardly progressive, these are merely the publicly acceptable face of a more audacious strategy. It is Irigaray's conviction that celebrating a morphology of the female body really is a significant challenge to dominant metaphysical systems that take their form from a phallic morphology.[6] There is an entirely other world that can be imagined. The eruption of the female body into cultural form signifies, for Irigaray, the possibility of a transforming hope. She writes, 'Something has been held in reserve within the silence of the feminine; an energy, a morphology, a growth and flourishing still to come from the female realm' (1993c: 19). In fact, in Irigaray's writing, the female sexed body becomes the most significant trope pointing to the sensible transcendental, an image of the divine which mediates between flesh and spirit. She articulates the potential this offers for revisioning a metaphysical system which has become deathly. Now there exists a remarkable opportunity to engage in the 'remaking of immanence and transcendence notably through this *threshold* which has not been examined as such: the female sex' (1993c: 18).

In a further striking parallel to Smart's vision, Irigaray also uses the figure of the female lover seeking her male partner, and their erotic reconciliation, to articulate her utopian faith. To the consternation of many feminists, the metaphor of heterosexual desire is employed to point towards an alternative social order in which sexed difference symbolizes the respect for alterity and the possibility of a sociality which does not seek to eradicate what it cannot subsume. Sexual desire is figured as divine yearning. Irigaray states, 'Love is the vehicle which permits a passage between the sensible and the transcendent, sensible and intelligible, mortal and immortal, above and below, immanent and transcendent' (1991: 164). If the male lover has betrayed this vision then the female lover must guard it the more, cherish the archaic knowledge of mutuality in the hope that this love can be reborn. The female lover still bears the trace of her male lover's caress. She retains faith as she carries its generative potential

---

[5]   See, for example, Irigaray (1993b).

[6]   This phallic symbolic order celebrates the unitary, the visible, the triumph of the one over the other. It secures its authority by obscuring its own origins and thus the repression of alterity is integral to the current regime of truth. Irigaray writes: 'Eclipse of the mother, of the place (of) becoming, whose non-representation or even disavowal upholds the absolute being attributed to the father. He no longer has any foundations, he is beyond all beginnings' (1985: 307).

into the future. 'This memory of the flesh … means ethical fidelity to incarnation. To destroy it is to risk the suppression of alterity, both the God's and the other's. Thereby dissolving any possibility of access to transcendence (1993c: 217).

Birthing the world again

In this brief exploration of the parallels between the work of Smart and Irigaray, the extent of their extreme faith becomes apparent. I have made connections between Smart and Irigaray not to enrol Smart as some proto-feminist poststructuralist but rather to challenge those of us who happily use Irigaray's symbolics as our common currency for everyday transactions. Irigaray has been massively influential but it is important to be clear about what are we doing and what are we saying when we employ her ideas and enter the space of her 'female imaginary'. Do we share the extreme faith that within the rhetorical space of female embodiment we can begin to create an alternative cultural/symbolic order? Do we believe, like Smart and Irigaray, that love can prove as strong as death? Really as strong? This kind of love? So many deaths? If we do not so believe then surely our discourse can be judged as a form of idealism? If we do so believe then are we prepared to be as radically audacious in our imagining as such a utopian vision requires?

These questions return me to the religious traditions which have shaped my vision of the world. Christian theologians and mystics through the centuries have seen the erotic metaphors of the Song of Songs as fitting to describe the love relation between Christ and humanity. Such love, the language of popular devotion has proclaimed, covers all ills, all pains. There is no sorrow, no dying any more, no injury too great but that this love can redeem it. Cancel it out. Smart and Irigaray's writing causes me to wrestle with these massive themes again. My imagination places the desiring and fertile woman in the space of the sacrificial male who is figured as redeemer. This enables me to contemplate the impossible mathematics of redemption anew. Can it be that this one love, this great desire, births the world again? Smart and Irigaray return to me the scandal, the madness and the mystery of extreme faith. *Love is as strong as death.*

Smart's poem 'Birth of a Child in Wartime' is a hymn of praise to the redemptive power of incarnate love in the body of a woman. In this, despite the gravity of the times, the fertile womb breaks the silence of despair and rejoices with a 'birth psalm'. Heaven approves this celebration and legions of angels cavort across the heavens like 'squadrons in a war apart', releasing indiscriminate loads of bliss, 'On everything that is' (1992c: 41).

Chapter 8

Sex in the War: An Aesthetics of Resistance in the Diaries of Etty Hillesum

The war diaries of Etty Hillesum have not been as widely read as those of her younger, and more famous, compatriot Anne Frank. Neither have they been 'canonized' as Holocaust literature in the same way. Although Etty (Esther) was also Jewish, and a brilliant chronicler of the terrifying events that led her to Auschwitz, extracts from her work and personal memorabilia are not preserved for public edification and the small room overlooking the Rijksmuseum where she sat and wrote has not become a memorial or shrine. Children are not encouraged to ponder the passages she composed in the knowledge that 'people are being killed at this very moment all over the world, while I sit here writing beside my rose-red cyclamen under my steel office lamp' (1999: 261). But perhaps it is not surprising that she has had to wait so many years to gain an audience for her vivid reflections when the published diaries begin like this:

> This is a painful and well nigh impossible step for me: yielding up so much that has been suppressed to a blank sheet of lined paper … It is like the final liberating scream that always sticks bashfully in your throat when you make love. I am accomplished in bed, just about seasoned enough I should think to be counted among the better lovers, and love does indeed suit me to perfection. (1999: 3)

It was the 9th of March, 1941. The Netherlands were occupied and the Nazi crackdown on the Jews was underway; ghettoes had been created and 'work camps' set up. A growing battery of regulations was gradually removing Jewish people from participation in civil life. 'I am accomplished in bed', Etty Hillesum wrote on the first page of her diary.

A space apart

Sex and war are frequently brought into correlation. In historical and literary accounts of conflict situations, we read how people surrounded by too much violence, death and dying try and fuck their way out – looking for an escape, a forgetfulness or oblivion in the sexual act. We also read many terrifying testimonies in which sex is used as another weapon of war. Rape and violation here function as highly effective methods of terror and control. I am aware, of course, of these very important conjunctions but they are not my concern in this chapter. What I am eager to explore here is something different. I am interested in how in the work of a number of women writers – Etty Hillesum is my focus here – sex comes to represent a contrasting space to the space of war.

Like war, sex is a physical space. Flesh touches flesh here. When the two are placed together, an immediate and obvious contrast emerges between bodily gestures which embrace, comfort and delight the other, and those which harm and destroy. But in the war journals of Etty Hillesum much more than this simple contrast is at work. Sex is very important in her writing. In its embodied particularity it comes to stand for the vivid instant: the radiant moment which transcends the total warfare in which she lived. Like the rose-red cyclamen she looks to as she writes, it is a point of active resistance that proves the existence of a contrary power. Every pretty blouse I put on is a victorious celebration, she affirms (1999: 196). The mundaneness and apparent triviality of each sensuous moment do not diminish its power:

> An old dress ... a little bit of sun ... One hand is all we need to caress. And a little work. And our work can be done anywhere, wherever there is a human being, be he only a camp guard. I am coming over to your place right now. I have put on a beauty of a new pink wool blouse, and I have washed myself from head to toe with lilac soap. (1999: 155)

Nor can the smallness of the erotic space reduce its significance:

> I once quietly bemoaned the fact that there is so little space for our physical love in your two small rooms, and no chance of going elsewhere because of all those notices and prohibitions. And now it seems like a virtual paradise of promise and freedom. Your little rooms, your small table lamp, my lilac soap and your caressing hands. God knows how much that means ... [for] all that may lie in store. (1999: 156)

Sex and poetry

So sex contests the space of war as a bright, vivid moment and testifies that all resistance is not yet overcome and, furthermore, constructed in this manner the act of love comes to represent the perseverance of beauty amongst so much that is barren, ugly and despoiled. In Hillesum's symbolic universe, sex stands at the heart of a continuum that links natural beauty, the jasmine on a sunny terrace (1999: 185), a summer day on the moors with tanned bare legs and gypsy hair (1999: 134) with literature, art and poetry – particularly the poetry of Rilke[1] – in a very material aesthetics. Hillesum was pursuing advanced studies in literature, languages and philosophy when the tide of war overtook her. She aspired to make her own mark upon European culture and firmly believed that what culture preserves as precious testifies to the resilience of beauty – a beauty that could not be obliterated by the most appalling historical circumstances and was as vital to life as air, food and sunshine – particularly so in the midst of suffering. 'Sadly,' she writes, 'in difficult times we tend to shrug off the spiritual heritage of artists from an "easier age"... It is an understandable but shortsighted reaction. And utterly impoverishing' (1999: 282). For Hillesum there are no false distinctions to be made between art and nature as they witness together to radiance at the heart of existence. There truly is heaven in a wild flower and, she scandalously affirmed, a poem is 'as real and as important as a young man falling out of an aeroplane' (1999: 50).

This faith was not easy to maintain. But although she constantly questioned whether her passions (intellectual and physical) could be justified, she discovered – in the folded-back sheets of a lover's bed and in the well-fingered sheets of a poetry book – a power that confronts/overcomes nihilism and death. 'I don't sit here in my peaceful flower-filled room, praising You through your poets and thinkers ... I try to face up to Your world, God, not escape from it ... And I continue to praise Your creation' (1999: 164–5). Her sensuous appreciation of life becomes increasingly important as she realizes that, for the condemned, art and beauty must now carry what politics and ethics can no longer bear. Although she never repudiated the left-wing convictions of her social circle, and was in active contact with resistance groups, these beliefs became increasingly hypothetical when facing a blank horizon. 'I said last night to twenty-one-year-old Hans "Look politics really isn't everything in life you know"' (1999: 91).

Hillesum knew that for the majority of Jews in the Netherlands there was no possibility of escape and to the despair of her friends she decided

---

[1]   The poet she turned to in her most difficult times and whose work she carried with her when she was deported.

that she would not seek a route out herself (Hoffman 1999 [1996]: xxv). But to live, rather than exist, confronting death it was necessary to lay claim to the beauty that overcomes hate. While anger and grief were inevitable emotions and resistance was necessary, she sought strength in an alternative vision as these extracts from her journal illustrate:

> Yes, the trees, sometimes at night their branches would bow down under the weight of the fruit of stars, and now they are menacing daggers piercing the bright spring air. Yet even in their new shape and setting they are beautiful ... I thought to myself, even if the whole of this world is bombed to bits, we shall build a new world, and that one too will pass, and still life will be beautiful, always beautiful. (1999: 117)

> ... life is beautiful and so rich it makes you want to believe in God. (1999: 119)

> I often see visions of poisonous green smoke; I am with the hungry, with the ill-treated and the dying, every day, but I am also with the jasmine and with that piece of sky beyond my window; there is room for everything in a single life. For belief in God and a miserable end. (1999: 186)

Belief in God was part of her material aesthetics – integral to it. One of the most striking and most compelling aspects of Hillesum's diaries is the journey she makes through erotic intimacies to passionate belief. As a student of European literature, philosophy and psychology, she concedes the dead weight of religious orthodoxy and the complaints that have often been made against beauty on the part of faith. She wryly acknowledges the difficulties caused by this cultural inheritance – particularly for women like herself, 'tied down and enmeshed in centuries old traditions and finding it difficult to be on equally good terms with God and your body' (1999: 42). Nevertheless, the path she follows leads through sensuous beauty and towards an erotic intimacy with the divine.

Sex and God

The spiritual awakening which enabled Hillesum to escape enmeshment in old traditions and discover an erotic path to God began in a love affair. However, this is not the familiar tale of the wayward one who is enlightened through the pure love of a good man/woman. Hillesum, the seasoned lover, was not sentimental concerning her sexual experience. There had been many intimate encounters: 'I have broken my body like bread and shared it out among men. And why not, they were hungry?' (1999: 281). The relationship through which she found herself dragged into a new awareness of God was an ambivalent, surreptitious and nonmonogamous relationship with a Jewish refugee from Berlin – Julius Spier. Spier was a Jungian psychoanalyst, palm reader and trained vocalist. His unorthodox method of therapy involved wrestling with his women patients, about which Hillesum sarcastically remarks, 'A funny way of treating patients you have, you get pleasure out of it and you get paid for it as well' (1999: 25). Amongst his many eccentricities Spier's idiosyncratic, syncretistic religious beliefs stood out. Despite her intellectual sophistication, Hillesum perceived that Spier had achieved a spiritual wisdom that she was lacking. When he became not only her lover but also her spiritual mentor she began to explore the significance of religious thought and embark upon her own mystical apprenticeship.

Intriguingly, it is the physical gestures of her lover before God that initially preoccupy her attention. As she prays she wishes to draw closer to Spier at prayer – to experience the pathos of intimacy:

> I know the intimate gestures he uses with women, but I still want to know the gestures he uses with God. Does he kneel down in the middle of his small room and what does he say? Does he kneel before he takes his dentures out or afterwards? (1999: 93)

Having been *a girl who could not kneel* she begins to find that the physical desire to pray increasingly overwhelms her. Astonishingly she finds herself falling to her knees as if compelled by a physical force. 'I suddenly found myself on the floor … And when Han came in and seemed a bit taken aback I told him I was looking for a button' (1999: 94). And through the influence of Spier, Etty learns not only to pray but to read the Bible. In the middle of these pious occupations Hillesum remains amusedly aware of the incongruity of it all. This is not the chaste convent cell lined with books, overlooking cornfields, which she had once coveted as an ideal place in which to achieve sublime wisdom (1999: 44). She and Spier were not holy innocents – quite the opposite!

> We have had wild and unfettered lives in many strange beds, and we are nevertheless shy again each time. I find this very beautiful and delight in it. Now I shall put on my brightly coloured dressing gown and go downstairs and read the Bible with him. (1999: 198)

Someone like me a lily of the field

A material aesthetics which finds God in a sexual embrace and reads the Bible in a brightly coloured dressing gown appears to be at odds with what the tangled webs of 'centuries old traditions' (Hillesum 1999: 42) have taught women about the relationship between their bodies and the sacred. In recent times feminist poststructuralist theorists (notably Luce

Irigaray)[2] have argued that both religion and politics will be transformed when the perpetually ambiguous female body becomes a source of sacred knowledge. Whilst feminist theologians have been quick to affirm women's bodily goodness, the ambivalence of female embodiment has been less frequently reflected upon. Writing some twenty years before the first feminist theologians, Hillesum reflects upon themes that are still often avoided by religious feminists. She does so with both insight and humour, transgressing many taboos.

Embodiment for Hillesum is both ecstatic and wearisomely painful. There are many times when gripped by headaches, fatigue or fear she wishes to transcend bodily limitations. Nevertheless, she recognizes that it is misguided for the spiritual seeker to withdraw from the sensory territory of the flesh. The body itself perceives the divine through its own mechanisms. Menstruation, for example, representing 'the interaction of body and soul is a most mysterious thing' (1999: 75). All sorts of apprehensions and visions are possible in the 'dreamy yet illuminating mood' she experiences when 'my lower anatomy is in a ferment' (1999: 76).

Another significantly ambivalent feature of Hillesum's representation of embodiment, that which is usually avoided in sanitized commentaries upon Hillesum's journals, is the abortion she carries out early in her relationship with Spier. It is discomforting to read her reflections upon this experience. She is swept away 'by all the fears of those young girls who suddenly realize they are expecting a baby' (1999: 85). She addresses the foetus, 'I am determined to leave you in a state of unbornness, rudimentary being that you are ... I shall fight patiently and relentlessly until you are once again returned to nothingness' (1999: 87–8). She has no regrets about her actions as 'the mothering instinct is something of which I am completely devoid' (1999: 85). Most challengingly she does not exclude the process of abortion, assaulting herself with hot water and blood-curdling instruments, from her increasingly close relationship with God. The whole process takes place in the time when she is becoming a person who kneels:

> I kneel once more on the coconut matting, my hands over my eyes and pray: 'O Lord let me feel at one with myself. Let me perform a thousand daily tasks with love, but let everyone spring from a greater central core of devotion and love.' Then it won't really matter what I do and where I am. But I still have a very long way to go. I shall swallow twenty quinine pills today; I feel a bit peculiar down there, south of my midriff. (1999: 85)

It is rare and disturbing to read an account of an abortion from someone who narrates their experience of this process not only before her readers

2   See, for example *Sexes and Genealogies* (Irigaray 1993a).

but before God. Hillesum herself wonders how the painful, inconvenient and 'senseless monthly performance' (1999: 75) she associates with female fertility can produce spiritual illumination. Her readers may find it difficult to imagine how she can rise from kneeling to take her twenty tablets of quinine in the serene confidence that 'despite this muddle concerning an unborn child ... it will all turn out all right' (1999: 86).

What continually challenges me is how Hillesum's ambivalent and very peculiar love affairs can have generated the profound conversations with God that mark the pages of her journal. Her companion Spier does not conform to the characteristics of either the good lover or the spiritual confessor. He is a flamboyant charlatan and he has false teeth. Furthermore, few of her female admirers acknowledge the fact that Hillesum was also sleeping with her 'employer', Han, and that her place in his household as a quasi-housekeeper raises many questions about how she understood the commerce of sexual intercourse. Clearly not in a conventional way. 'I had an exhilarating walk with S. I am really faithful to him, inwardly. I am faithful to Han as well. I am faithful to everyone' (1999: 87).

But reading Hillesum's provocative and funny accounts of her relationships forces me to the recognition that she is only writing in large letters what most of us experience in our intimate lives but probably address in lower case. Sexual love is always unruly and perverse because ambivalence is what characterizes our sexual selves. Lovers never embody the ideal forms of platonic beauty. They are annoying, imperfect and they get old. There is no sexual relationship that is solely based on the gift of the self to the other. Calculation is always part of the encounter. Children are both the blessing and the curse of love. Real sex, real bodies, real passions are deeply flawed and always mixtures of light and shadow. But this does not mean, Hillesum demonstrates to us, that they must either be purged of their imperfections or set aside: '"O God, I thank you for having created me as I am ... I promise you to try and strive my whole life long for beauty and harmony and also humility and true love." And now to clear the breakfast table ... and put a little paint on my face' (1999: 90).

As I read and re-read the moving shapes of light and shadow, the sacred and the everyday, that fill the pages of Hillesum's journals, they recall for me the wild beauty of the Gospel narratives. In these too innocence and experience, small birds and flowers, and the extreme passions of wounded bodies, are displayed together in a vivid tableau. Reading Hillesum returns me to the Bible. Not because I like to imagine her reading it in her brightly coloured dressing gown (although I do) but because she reminds me of the bitter sweetness of the Gospels from which she quotes repeatedly towards the end of her life. Sometimes this is in the spirit of self-admonishment: 'My latest treasure the birds of heaven and the lilies of the field ... But seek ye first the kingdom of heaven' (1999: 260). Always she addresses the text with humour, considering herself to be a very strange disciple:

with a shirt on my back and another in my rucksack, a very small Bible, my Russian dictionary, Tolstoy's folk tales and no doubt, no doubt at all one volume of Rilke's letters. And then the pure lambswool sweater ... what a lot of possessions I have, oh God, and someone like me wants to be a lily of the field. (1999: 256)

Something has crystallized

I have argued that for Hillesum 'sex in the war' represents a vivid moment of freedom that escapes the violence of her times. I have shown that in her erotic aesthetics sex belongs with natural beauty and artistic production and that these together confront the ugliness of historical circumstances. Her material aesthetics contains its own sensuous appreciation of the divine – an appreciation that is marked by ambiguity and ambivalence but which is nevertheless vibrant and resilient. Hers is a spirituality of light and shadow. With painful clarity she affirms the need to acknowledge both beauty and horror in religious life. There must be room for everything, 'for belief in God and a miserable end' (1999: 86). I now turn to the later pages of her journal and the reflections that she makes on the last stage of her spiritual journey in which her understanding of beauty and passion achieve a new and profound form.

In the early writings Hillesum frequently expresses her own wonder that the world of war and the space of erotic delight can coexist, as these two passages illustrate:

> I lay on that bed, for the first time naked in his arms ... he thought me beautiful. And placed his hand carefully on my breast and whispered almost with surprise 'So soft'. And how gentle ...
> The threat grows ever greater and terror increases from day to day. (1999: 163)

> ... from my bed I stared out through the large open window. And it was once more as if life with all its mysteries were close to me, as if I could touch it. I had a feeling that I was resting against the naked breast of life and could feel her gentle regular heart beat ... And I thought, how strange it is war time. There are concentration camps. (1999: 165)

What happens later – as the country walks with Spier cease, as the parks are closed to Jews, as bicycles are forbidden and the systematic deportations begin – is that the world's space contracts. The two small rooms for loving, the square of sky from her window, the smell of jasmine, the camp that awaits her, the fate that awaits her; the two universes fuse. It is no longer that sexual delight preserves the space for freedom in the war. It is rather that a vivid beauty has come to irradiate all the space she inhabits. She no longer escapes into an alternative world:

> What they are after is our total destruction. I know it now ... living and dying, sorrow and joy, the jasmine behind the house, the persecution, the unspeakable horrors – it is all as one to me and I accept it as one mighty whole something has crystallized. (1999: 189)

Something has crystallized. There is a chemical change evidenced in the second half of the journal. In a poignant passage Hillesum reflects upon the jasmine flowers that have sustained her faith. These have been battered by storms and now lie grey and torn in muddy puddles on the ground:

> But somewhere inside me the jasmine continues to blossom undisturbed, just as profusely and delicately as it ever did. And it spreads its scent round the house in which you dwell O God. You can see I look after you. I bring you not only my tears and forebodings on this stormy, grey Sunday morning. I even bring you scented jasmine. (1999: 219)

A similar but greater loss occurs in her personal life. Spier escapes his imminent deportation but only because he dies suddenly and prematurely. Bereaved of his flesh Hillesum comes to see that her fingers, the fingers of a more or less seasoned lover, must now reach out and touch the living flesh that is the embodiment of her times. She can feel the contours of the moment with her fingertips 'among the barracks of hunted and persecuted people' (1999: 255). She touches this in the transit camp, surrounded by glorious fields of purple lupins, where poetry is written and recited and where women grow tomatoes to feed to their babies. This is also the place where a deaf and dumb pregnant woman is brutally bundled into a truck and a Jewish man in fear and hatred bullies and abuses his colleagues like a camp guard. Amongst these wonders and humiliations the same sense of an intimate embrace of human life is manifest. There is nothing that cannot be touched.

What remains from wartime loving

It will be evident that I am deeply engaged by Hillesum's writing. I am in love with her humour, her eroticism, her material aesthetics, her sex-in-the-war way to God. However, it is not only because her journals make such compelling reading that I am addressing her work in this chapter. Nor is it simply that I hope to contribute to the growing awareness of the importance of her writing. It is rather because her work helps me to struggle with a question that remains as important today as it did when she smelled the jasmine, ran downstairs in her brightly coloured dressing gown and wrote her last postcard from the train carrying her East to Poland. Namely, how do we contemplate beauty and acknowledge suffering before God? Or what is the relation between aesthetics and suffering in the divine economy.

This is not my question alone. Many other theologians and critical theorists are addressing similar themes. I came to Hillesum's journals through reading the work of Hélène Cixous. Since the early 1980s Cixous has been preoccupied with addressing the relationship between a material aesthetics (which brings into conjunction the body/sexual desire/material/maternal origins/poetry in a similar way to that envisaged by Hillesum) and politics; the obligation to those who suffer.

This question is addressed in numerous works of poetry, fiction and criticism. For example, in *Lemonade: Everything Was So Infinite* (1994a) the narrator seeks to write a true love letter in the middle of a war. In the context of a state of perpetual hostility (what she refers to as a war against women and other living beings) the narrator learns that 'it was only in the beginning that Paradise was a garden with a precise address. But ever since then it can take place at any moment ... It's a state of joy' (1994a: 110). This state can be entered into at any moment even in the midst of the most appalling circumstances: '"having paradise" is not impossible because "being in paradise" does not mean having your residence there; it means knowing you can return there. Even during a war' (1994a: 110). It is the writers, mystics, artists and lovers who keep the garden open. They are the guardians of the sacred.

This is Cixous' conviction but an unease remains. Is love enough? Is joy enough? It is with this sense of unresolvement that Cixous turns in her university seminars to the work of Paul Celan, the Russian poet Osip Mandelstam and to Etty Hillesum. She is seeking in concrete historical figures evidence that body/love/ writing/poetry endures and is significant in the face of the most intense suffering. The question is not really can we write poetry after Auschwitz, she argues, confronting Adorno, but can we write poetry in Auschwitz and what difference does it make that we can? Hillesum, who prayed that the little bit of God in her might grow into poetry because a camp needs a poet who experiences life even there as a bard and is able to sing about it (1999: 274), offers evidence that creative resistance matters. Hillesum, who declared that despite everything 'I always return to Rilke' (1999: 281), is a source of renewed faith and hope – as well as a crucial resource in an ongoing attempt to construct a political poesis (material aesthetic passionate resistance) which goes beyond the hard/cold systems of a politics that is so easily turned against the vulnerable flesh.

Cixous is still working on this agenda, turning to the same question again and again in works like *Three Steps on the Ladder of Writing* (1993), *Manna* (1994b) and *Stigmata* (1998) – and I must say that I do not think she has come up with a resolvement as such (or that Hillesum did) but rather that she has creatively marked out a sacred territory. Increasingly Cixous' work becomes more religious and she turns to the Bible to provide the imagery and ancient resonances that deepen the questions she answers and the insights she shares. It seems that God inevitably gets caught up in the relation between beauty and politics, a fact that Hillesum's diaries gloriously affirm.

Chapter 9

The Gender of the Cyborg

The ethical and political task rests in a better understanding of the social
interests and future aspirations that lie behind these various depictions of
the post/human future. (Graham 2002: 37)

In offering this critical examination of cultural representations of the
post/human through the figure of the cyborg I have structured my
thoughts around two key questions articulated in Elaine Graham's
important text, *Representations of the Post/human*, 2002. The first of
these is what can we learn of the mechanisms of power through an examination of dominant cultural symbols? In other words, how are particular
identities, practices and privileges confirmed by the representational practices
evident in technical innovations and cultural fabulations? The second
question is can the processes of cultural production through which human
beings construct themselves and their world become transformative for us?
Here I am seeking to discern whether the material practices of symbolization
which have generated the cyborg might aid us in the construction of new
social visions, political practices and theological thinking.

The emphasis placed in this chapter upon the gender of the cyborg
serves to situate these two questions within the arena of sexual politics.
Thus my specific concern will be to ask in what way do representations
of the cyborg confirm certain gender identities and sexual practices?
And can the cyborg offer the potential to challenge our binary and hierarchical understandings of masculinity and femininity through the radical
challenge it represents to all essentialist constructions of human nature?

A postmodern icon

Cyborgs appear in many forms today. Their ubiquitous presence is felt
whenever the boundaries that separate the human from the machine are

breached and the conventions of 'ontological hygiene' (Graham 2002: 33–5) are compromised. Many feminists would claim that these cyborgs are not only present everywhere but are active and working to sustain the representational practices through which gender is enduringly inscribed within our culture. Anne Balsamo argues that cyborgs are in fact *the* 'postmodern icon', produced within a culture which is saturated by a technological male imaginary and that 'the dominant representation of cyborgs reinserts us into the dominant ideology by reaffirming bourgeois notions of human, machine and femininity' (1999: 154).

There are many arguments that can be made to support this. On the most basic level it is clear that our most mundane experiences of cyborg practice, when we reach beyond our flesh through the computer keyboard, are gendered. Research indicates boys enjoy losing themselves in the world of virtual reality and see the machine as a quasi-living entity with which they can form a passionate relationship. Girls are more likely to see their computers as tools aiding them in better interpersonal communication. Perhaps more worrying than this differentiated experience is the fact that the virtual worlds our computers provide access to have become yet other sites of violence against women. In the ubiquitous availability of pornography on the internet the 'real time' violation of girls and women is transformed into a virtual commodity. This can be purchased, swapped or secretly traded in an unholy exploitation of an elision between human flesh and screen image. There is also a growing awareness that sexual harassment is routinely experienced by women in online discussions, fantasy games and via email. The chat room can be as much a 'male space' as the boardroom and the dangers this presents to girls and women are becoming increasingly apparent.

If we begin to look beyond the interface with the computer and turn to popular cultural representations of the cyborg, we find that many of these also extend into our imagined futures the dominant gendered forms of today. From the comic book to the screen mediums, we are all familiar with representations of cyborgs that exaggerate and heighten, pleasurably and creatively or crudely and violently, the representations of gender already in circulation. From *Metropolis* to James Bond, from *Stepford Wives* (one and two) to *The Terminator*, gender representations are the means through which the significance of human identity in a technological future is experimented with, tested out and retransmitted. Male and female figures play familiar roles in these productions. To be sure, as Jenny Wolmark has argued, feminist science fiction has created cyborg images that 'reorder boundaries and demolish polarities' (1999b: 237). And yes, as she has argued further, the strong women characters in some cyberpunk fictions and film owe much to these feminist interventions (1999a: 142). We might even concede that male cyborgs through their hypermasculinity do queer themselves – or as Lois McNay would have it, 'fetishized images of masculinity bear within themselves traces of the feminized man transvestite and thus point towards their own constitutive instability and displacement' (2000: 55). It is nevertheless the case that gender stereotypes are more likely to be reaffirmed than challenged by the majority of cultural depictions of the post/human. As Mary Doane writes:

> Although it is certainly true that in the case of some contemporary science fiction writers – particularly feminist authors – technology makes possible a destabilisation of sexual identity as a category there has also been a curious but fairly insistent history of representations of technology which work to fortify sometimes desperately conventional understandings of the feminine. (In Balsamo 1999:148)

Female abjection

It is not remarkable that cyborg images have become part of the desperate work to sustain conventional gender categories. Popular cultural icons are not only compelling because of their novelty but precisely because they return us via modern vehicles to classic sites of cultural tension and anxiety. This is made very clear in Graham's writing on monsters, the golem and the cultural prehistory of the cyborg. These sites of stress are where what Julia Kristeva (1982) has termed 'the powers of horror' and the mechanisms of female abjection are most clearly discerned and reproduced. This reminds us, contra to much of the more optimistic literature on cyborgs, that the boundary territory or border where identity is contested is not always a happy place of delightful confusion. It is also the site where stands a 'victimising machine at the cost of which I become the subject of the symbolic as well as the other of the abject' (Kristeva 1982: 112). This victimizing mechanism is the means through which social anxieties are resolved through the re-production of subjectivities in conformity with a phallogocentric symbolic order that cannot tolerate the disruptive indeterminacy of the feminine.[1]

Many of our most enduring cultural anxieties are related to the need to achieve mastery over the threat to social order posed by the baleful forces of the feminine sphere. These primal fears and the mechanisms for their overcoming are rehearsed again for us in cyborg dramas. Many of these are concerned with the ambivalence of maternal power and the necessity to achieve discreet subjectivity through relinquishing the maternal connection. Kristeva has a vivid metaphor for the abjection of

---

[1] The 'feminine' in Kristeva's work is the unspeakable, embodied realm where identities are confused and chaotic libidinal forces threaten to annihilate subjectivity and the social order.

the maternal by the subject who seeks individuation through repudiation of identity with the mother. She describes it as vomiting milk (1982: 3–4). This is enacted in *The Matrix* where the one who is to come is detached from his cyborg continuity with the maternal nexus that feeds him, nurtures him and incorporates his identity and vital force. He spews white fluid.

Overlapping anxieties to those concerning maternal power are articulated around issues concerning human reproduction. This is an area where many deep fears are situated concerning personal origins, individuation, continuity, familial and sexual authority, ethnicity, the dispersion of property and the continuation of the species – to name but a few! The cyborg bears these concerns into the popular imagination for, as *Bladerunner* famously illustrates, no cyborg has a mummy but they do possess the potential for endless replication. Once again the threats cyborgs present to our discrete humanity (ontological hygiene) are frequently feminized. The cyborg temptress may seduce the real man or the frail woman may be a less vigilant defender of ontological hygiene than her male partner. This is the case in Steven Spielberg's truly awful film *AI* in which the mother character is presented as a source of weakness that may lead to the adulteration of the species. She is more amenable to loving the replicant, the 'mecha' child, whereas the father's concerns are for his own damaged but authentic 'human' son.

It is not only in the popular representation of cyborg characters that gender signifiers alert us to deep social unease. The cyborg sphere of existence, this real-becoming-virtual world, is also commonly portrayed as a feminine space. It is imaged as a place of fascination, illusion, pleasure, loss of self. Here we lose our human freedom, and are confined in a docile servitude. Nicola Nixon, writing on cyberpunk, speaks of a feminized universe inhabited by ghosts (1999: 199). In the film *The Matrix* this imagery is striking as human creatures are plugged into their nurturing but destructive captivity. And in Cronenberg's *eXistenZ* we are captivated by Allegra, the dangerous queen of gaming and her organic, fleshly game pod (which Graham has likened to breasts but which I see as placental) that leads us innocents into a place of foul flesh and abasement.

The contrast between real world/feminized world made here is interesting because it is only relatively recently in Western culture that this everyday world of material and social relations has been seen as real – rather than as a cave of illusions, daydreams and enchantments from which we shall emerge into an ideal reality. I am using the language here of Plato's cavern which Irigaray, in *Speculum of the Other Woman* (1985: 345), famously demonstrated to be a material feminized space and which Kristeva reinscribed as the chora, receptacle and womb. What is evident is that whether imaged as material or virtual the place of inauthenticity and illusion is the feminized space. Many of the apocalyptic representations of post/human futures in contemporary culture return us directly to the sedimented symbolics of gynophobia in their most archaic forms.

Cyborg politics

In responding to Graham's challenge to interrogate the power relations that constitute contemporary cultural forms I have identified a number of ways in which the old worlds of gender inequality, real and symbolic violence against women are being rearticulated through cyborg forms. In so doing I have moved from questions concerning social relations to issues relating to the binary divisions that lie at the heart of the Western symbolic order. The cyborg moves easily through these two realms which are still too often viewed as different spheres of analysis between which theoretical forms of ontological hygiene still prevail. Many feminist thinkers continue to take oppositional stances and focus either upon the life experiences of real women or, alternatively, upon what poststructuralism identifies as the feminine; that which lacks cultural representation (loss, absence, death, desire, indeterminacy, etc.). However, poststructuralist feminists such as Rosi Braidotti (1991) and Alice Jardine (1985) have long argued that current interest in the feminine as that which is excluded and marginalized in our binary and hierarchical symbolic system was provoked precisely by the rise of feminist politics. The work of Simone de Beauvoir on woman as other or Virginia Woolf on women and writing was widely debated within the women's movement and provoked the beginnings of an epistemological shift the resonance of which is evident, if unacknowledged, in later poststructuralist writing. Linda Curti argues that feminists must claim these genealogical connections because the postmodern weakening of the unitary human subject may have been brought about by the very existence of feminist and female thought (1998: 10). De Lauretis argues that a dual focus on 'women' as the subject of real historical relations and 'woman' as culture's other enables us to understand the mechanisms of the 'technologies of gender' (1987: 6). The figure of the cyborg who so clearly moves between these worlds of material/social relations and symbolic representations reveals not only that they are not separate realms but also that the technologies of gender sustain them equally. Some feminists have also suggested that the cyborg points us towards the possibility that the mechanism might be jammed. The binary code broken.

More optimistic feminist thinking on this issue owes so much to Donna Haraway and in particular her generative essay, 'A Cyborg Manifesto' (1991b). Graham lucidly expounds Haraway's thinking in what is personally my favourite chapter of her book, 'Cyborg Writing'. She quotes Haraway's brilliant phrase the cyborg tells us of the 'inextricable weave of the organic, technical, textual, mythic, economic and political threads that make up the flesh of the world' (Haraway, in Graham 2002: 202) and goes on to explore how the rhetorical figure of the cyborg breaches the codes of ontological hygiene by rendering unstable the boundaries between humans, animals and machines.

However, it is not only species boundaries which Haraway's cyborg challenges. It also points to the dissolution of the foundational dualisms, gendered at root, through which we have explained ourselves to ourselves in the past. When all such essentialist categories are critiqued, Haraway believes the possibility emerges for new forms of political intervention. No longer are we separated by discrete identities assumed to be inviolable, nor are we locked into nostalgic longings for what is authentic, natural or pure. We can now engage in cyborg political practices that demonstrate no fear of syncretism, miscegenation or adultery. Haraway envisions the emergence of a cyborg politics which is based upon an 'infidel heteroglossia' in which illicit relations between diverse groups take place in order to achieve strategic forms of social regeneration rather than perfect redemption.

This is a revisioning of politics that is appealing to women who have come to suspect that claims to innocence, moral purity and political integrity are themselves bloody weapons of mass destruction bringing the natural/technological/human flesh of our world to the brink of disaster. These political imaginings are particularly attractive if the cyborg falls both within and beyond what has been designated the space of woman. Haraway's cyborg is always female but not woman, 'always a girl who's trying not to become Woman' (Haraway, in Graham 2002: 207). She delights in the confusion her indeterminacy generates within established political traditions. It is easy to respond to the contagious optimism this cyborg generates for some feminists. Not only does she represent women no longer alienated from the historical/technological processes that shape our world, but her post/human form is more resilient than our frail flesh. When we are defeated she adapts. When we are wounded she mutates. When we confront chasms between good and evil, faith and despair, she has achieved the sacral status of those revered beings that carry our contradictions within themselves.

However, it is also plain why this post/human figure is an anathema to other women activists. Feminist politics are marked by what Curti has described as a nostalgic 'preoccupation with the abandonment of the real, particularly the political real' (1998: 1). The reality check of this nostalgic feminism is the figure of the flesh-and-blood woman in living relation with others and suffering material oppression. It is against the representations of this figure (who is also a cultural fabulation) that all feminist interventions are judged. What is to be feared is that her needs will be neglected by those who are supposed to be dedicated to her emancipation as they are seduced by other, more trivial but superficially engaging, concerns. It is not going to be easy to persuade feminists (particularly religious feminists and feminist theologians) to relinquish this icon and embrace silicon skin. And perhaps the nostalgia Curti correctly identifies within contemporary feminism for the real struggles of real women should be viewed as a legitimate defensive reaction to the illusion that transformed political futures are easily achieved through processes of cultural change and resymbolization. Surely the mechanisms of power which have regulated sexual relations in the past so effectively are not so easily transformed?

This question can be considered more closely if we examine the link that is now routinely made (as any viewer of the *X-Men* series of films will be aware) between the post/human and the queer.

The cyborg and the queer

Like cyborg politics, queer theory celebrates the destabilization of identity decentring the regulative norms of heterosexuality. Feminist, gay and lesbian identities thus become as amorphous as they were once perverse. In my editorial work for the journal *Theology and Sexuality* I routinely review articles that refer to 'translesbigays' or LGBTs and also come across texts written by 'heterosexual queers'. Many feminists have argued that whilst the queering of identity offers a welcome challenge to essentialist understandings of gender and sexuality, it also effectively undermines struggles to assert distinct spheres of knowledge, experience and resistance. It also tends to deflect attention away from contesting the economic, legal and moral boundaries that sustain heteronormativity. These can be safely held in place while we experiment with transgressive performances which may well call into question what is normal, natural or chosen in sexual identity but do little to shift the balance of power.

Such arguments suggest that the cyber/queer embracing of indeterminacy, libidinal transgression and ludic innovation may not be the only or best resource we have to challenge the established and violent forms of sexual regulation. Yes, of course such performative interventions do have significance – the politics of pleasure is important – but it is also the case that dominant cultural forms are effectively safeguarded by the tolerance of multiple marginalized alternatives that offer no serious challenges to their hegemonic power. As McNay argues, the parodic performance of gender roles is only subversive or disruptive within communal contexts predisposed to the dissolution of hegemonic identities. 'In other contexts the same reinscription can serve to re-idealize rather than denaturalize heterosexual norms' (2000: 61). We need only to think of the distinction between the over-the-top performance of gender roles at Carnival or at Pride and compare these with the over-the-top performance of gender roles within the Catholic Church to see the force of her argument.

I am following McNay further. In her important book *Gender and Agency* (2000), which interestingly features a picture of a female cyborg on the front cover, she concedes one of the most central tenets of Graham's text – namely that we can no longer sustain a distinction between material struggles and symbolic ones. However, she questions whether we overestimate the instability of symbolic forms and thus exaggerate the effects of alternative practices of representation, parodic performance and new libidinal economies. I remember in the dismal days of Thatcher and Reagan we took some comfort from the work of cultural theorists who suggested that although traditional class militancy appeared in decline the spirit of resistance could still be discerned in subcultural identities and everyday forms of resistance: tattoos, dreadlocks, punk rock, the housewives experiential knowledge in conflict with media representations of ideal femininity. Some twenty years on it is important to recognize that there were important insights being articulated here about how politics has mutated in our lifetimes. Nevertheless it is also important to concede that these forms of resistance were not able seriously to challenge the order under which we live now. Is the blurring of boundaries and transgressive indeterminacy represented through the cyborg any more powerful than those counter-hegemonic cultural forms in which left-wing intellectuals invested so heavily in former times? If this is the case it will be because, as *Representations of the Post/human* argues, the metaphor is so central to the cultural narratives (scientific and mythological) that shape our world today.

Cyborg theology

It has been my concern up to this point to demonstrate the various, and frequently conflicting, political concerns that are currently being articulated through the figure of the cyborg and to assess their significance for feminist politics. I have sought to demonstrate the importance of enquiring into the power relations that are replicated by current cultural trends whilst also being open to their subversive potential.

For Graham, representations of the post/human serve to mirror enduring anxieties, provide the means to explore technological innovation and enable us to see beyond current possibilities. She writes, 'Fantastic representations of the post/human offer important insights into the many meanings of being human but they are also devices by which new worlds can be imagined (2002: 234). This judgement expresses a (very) cautious optimism concerning the potential of cyborg politics. However, Graham is a highly creative theologian as well as a cultural critic. What are the features of 'cyborg theology' that can be discerned in her work?

Like cyborg politics, cyborg theology will also be concerned with breaching categories of ontological hygiene and enquiring into the validity of distinctions previously maintained between matter and spirit, immanence and transcendence, humanity and God. In the closing pages of *Representations of the Post/human*, Graham presents an evocative picture of the possibilities for Christian practice that emerge once we have learned to view transcendence not as that which sets us apart from God but as that which moves us beyond 'the ontological hygiene of fixed essences into realising new, as yet unarticulated possibilities for identity and community' (2002: 219). The divine that provokes this movement is expressed 'through the medium of embodied, contingent experience' (2002: 233). Graham is reaching towards a profoundly sacramental awareness which fuses the material practices of human life with a sacred horizon.

It is clear that the theological perspective Graham is advocating has a great many positive features – particularly for women. As feminists from de Beauvoir onwards have grasped, a binary system that divides spirit from matter, mind from body and the sacred from the profane also places men on one side and women on the other. There are enduring theological traditions within, that place women and men in ontologically differentiated relations to transcendence. Cyborg theologies that synthesize divine and human horizons effectively challenge the legitimacy of such concepts which always locate women in a darker and dirtier space than men. Furthermore, Graham is robust in her assertions that it is part of the duty of the theologian not merely to transmit models of transcendence that legitimate technoscientific power but to change them. If representations of the post/human offer the potential to jam the technologies of gender, can they not also break the binary codes opening the way to better understandings of divine and human nature?

I am largely in sympathy with Graham's thinking on these issues and cherish no illusions concerning the innocence of the tradition or its impact upon women. However, I am uneasy about a significant problem that emerges if cyborg politics and theology encourage us to loosen our grasp upon notions of difference and alterity in order to embrace an indeterminacy that might too easily become manipulated by us. Diane Prosser (1995) warns against the conviction, dear to some constructive theologians, that we can periodically rearrange our religious symbolics into more ethically acceptable forms as moral conventions change. Religious traditions are more awkward and intransigent than that and the process of their renewal is much more painful. We are working within theological and cultural forms that fight back against our attempts to re-form them. However, their intractability has also been a means of preserving some resources we may need for social transformation.

Binary hierarchical symbolic systems are not a good thing but within them lurk notions of alterity and eradicable difference which escape containment. I don't think that radical difference has ever been particularly attractive to Graham and, re-reading her first book *Making the*

Difference: Gender, Personhood and Theology (1995), I see this to be the case. A preoccupation with difference as an ontological given would deflect us from an enquiry into how difference is actually generated and sustained. In *Representations of the Post/human* all that is alien is ultimately only 'our refracted other', much closer than we think, and of course the cyborg (the queer?) is not the other but ourself.

I sympathize with Graham's rejection of a God who is foreign to our embodied nature or transcendent in the sense of standing over against the world. But radical alterity does keep any possibility of change alive. This is why Jean-François Lyotard (1988) argues that within the post/human must be maintained the potentiality of engendered being and the desire for the w/holy other which provokes change. Irigaray, whose work Graham ably uses to support her quest for a God not foreign to the female flesh, bases her faith in the possibility of radical transformation upon a notion of ontological gender difference that keeps the system open (1993b: 41).

I am sure that Graham recognizes ambivalence in her thinking here and is careful to stress that there must always be certain instability in our cyborg visions. This is made apparent in her determination to retain the oblique stroke between post and human. In response to this oblique homage to alterity I would like to reaffirm that the sacramental sensibility she celebrates entails an understanding that we do not encounter in these mysteries a synthesis of the spiritual and material but their impossible communion. I would like to stress that the metaphors do not stabilize and unite ontologically different entities but that their conjunction generates a massive surge of illumination. I would wish to affirm that the work of a theologian is to wrestle with a stubbornly intractable tradition that can occasionally be brought to generate new forms. I also wish to welcome this cyborg who is a girl – and to entertain the possibility that there may be a ghost in this machine.

Chapter 10

A World Built on Water: Symbols of the Divine in the Novels of Marilynne Robinson

Massive critical attention is generated when a significant writer publishes a major new work after a long break. If the author has only written two novels this interest is particularly intense and comparisons are quickly drawn between the two books. *Housekeeping* (1981) and *Gilead* (2005a) by Marilynne Robinson are separated by a generation of literary silence.[1] Both books have won major prizes and are celebrated for their panoramic vision and poignant evocations of a world entire within a world. However, *Housekeeping* and *Gilead* are very different works; so dissimilar in fact that the space between them is loud with debate. Are the differences between the books best understood as resulting from a focus upon different aspects of human experience – or do they explore the same existential concerns from different angles? Does *Gilead* represent a turning away from the tragic vision of *Housekeeping* and a return to orthodoxy? Is *Housekeeping* a moral fable and *Gilead* a nostalgic romance?

Whilst it is widely acknowledged that Robinson is a deeply religious writer (see, for example, Ryan 2005), these questions are rarely given a sharp theological focus. However, I think that it is Robinson's religious understanding that gives each book it particular character and through which the links between them can be most fruitfully explored.

---

[1] But only literary silence. As well as teaching and speaking Robinson has also written two controversial works of non-fiction: *Mother Country* (1989) and *The Death of Adam* (2005b [1998]).

Housekeeping offers a disturbing view of the divine which is traced in the female sphere of intimate familial relationships (Robinson in Schaub 1994: 233). It portrays a world in which the boundaries have been breached. There are no bulwarks strong enough to secure our safety, separate the living from the dead or divide the realm of the sacred from that of small and perishable creatures. This is a novel in which nothing is permanent or established and its pages are flooded with a transcendence that breaks all human bounds.

In contrast *Gilead* has been heralded as an optimistic text. Its 'balm', critics have argued, flows from a loving celebration of all that is best in American religion. Its narrator John Ames, an elderly clergyman, is inheritor of both his grandfather's militant, evangelical radicalism, and his father's rational piety and abhorrence of violence. The God of *Gilead* is the God of Calvin,[2] Barth and Bonhoeffer.[3] This God understands that 'his' best lovers are the deepest doubters and the faith inscribed on its pages is open-minded as well as open-hearted. It is also enduring. Whilst Ames himself journeys towards death, and the town of Gilead slowly declines with him, there are still running strong and renewing streams of grace. Faith, hope and love remain – and much, much else besides.

These brief pen portraits of the spiritual dimensions of each book would tend to suggest that the novels stand a heaven's breadth as well as a whole generation apart. But the divine that appears as a deluge in *Housekeeping* and the Christian God who refreshes like spring rains in *Gilead* are linked by Robinson's sustained use of water imagery in both novels. In fact the special quality of Robinson's writing lies in the way she opens up small, personal narratives to become investigations of ultimate concerns through the conscious deployment of deep metaphors. She concedes that this way of writing locates her influences in an epoch very different from our own but argues that we require instruments now widely held to be obsolete if we are to be as adventurous as our prede-cessors in the spiritual exploration of human life:

> When you look at the older writers like Melville, and Thoreau and Emerson who were very influential for me in the way they used metaphor – and William Faulkner also is a very good example of the same thing – this deep integral use of metaphor as a means of accessing experience.

---

[2] See Robinson 2005b: 12.
[3] In an interview with Jill Owens, Robinson states:

> Karl Barth is the great theologian of the twentieth century, or of many centuries. And Dietrich Bonhoeffer is wonderful. They're very classical in the sense of speaking out of a very large conception of reality in part because of their circum-stances, as they were both anti-Hitler people in Germany. All kinds of ethical issues are very sharp for both of them, which is something that I really appreciate. They're not feel-good theologians. (Owens 2007)

That's the thing that I've really admired ... I've been influenced by it.
(Owens 2007)

Words about water

The influences we can identify in Robinson's use of water as a 'deep
metaphor' are ones she freely acknowledges. Nominating *Moby Dick* as
her favourite novel (Schaub 1994: 239), she locates herself in that tradition
in American writing that draws upon the sea and its creatures to describe
that dangerous and ungovernable element that extends our desires beyond
limits and exposes both the grandeur and frailty of our human
endeavours. This element can be variously named God or nature or fate.
By whatever name it is called it is experienced as overwhelming. This is
a tradition perpetuated in another sea-story that Robinson admires. In
Kate Chopin's *The Awakening* (1988 [1899]) the hero, Edna, awakens
to her own creative powers when she risks learning to swim. This
discovery propels her into passion, self-knowledge and a new kind of faith.
It also ultimately, but perhaps triumphantly, leads to her personal annihi-
lation. In her introduction to the text Robinson argues that as Edna
moves towards her tragic destiny she at last encounters the 'essence' of
her life:

> In discovering herself Edna is discovering her fate. In exploring Edna's
> regression, as she puts aside adult life, retracing her experience to its
> beginnings, for her its essence, Chopin describes as well a journey inward,
> evoking all the prodigal richness of longing, fantasy, and memory. The
> novel is not a simulated case study, but an exploration of the solitary soul
> still enchanted by the primal, charged, and intimate encounter of naked
> sensation with the astonishing world. (1988: xx)

The work of Ralph Waldo Emerson has also been deeply integrated into
Robinson's symbolic repertoire. Tace Hedrick states that it is from
Emerson that *Housekeeping* derives 'its most powerful image. The
mutable and englobing nature of water' (1999: 6). It is certainly true that
liquid images are everywhere in Emerson. In his essay 'Circles', for
example, he states, 'There are no fixtures in nature. The universe is fluid
and volatile' (1979 [1841]: 179). He then proceeds to suggest that God
takes a view of our world that affirms its constant flux and dynamic
motion. 'Our globe seen by God is a transparent law not a mass of facts.
The law dissolves the facts and holds it fluid' (1979 [1841]: 179). It is not
possible to explore the many ways in which Emerson has influenced
Robinson in the context of this essay. However, it is important to
emphasize that these extend beyond borrowing an important image from
an admired mentor. What particularly appeals to Robinson is Emerson's

capacity for analogical thinking. Emerson views nature as the site where humanity, through hard wrestling with intractable elements, achieves self-understanding and learns of God. Nature provokes us to wonder; it provides the symbols through which we begin to reason and to speak and, rightly understood, it communicates the mind of its creator. It even opens up for us the possibility of participation in the life of the divine. For Emerson there are no natural elements, no tides and motions, that do not participate in analogous relations with spiritual realities. These are sentiments affirmed by Robinson on numerous occasions:

> The world expresses the ultimate. (Robinson, in Schaub 1994: 249)

> To me everything that is beautiful about humankind is generated absolutely out of its response to the questioning difficulty that is generated out of the world, I think that a true understanding of what a human being *is* based on an understanding of this rapt conversation in which people are *all* engrossed (Robinson, in Schaub 1994: 251).

> So I have spent my life watching, not to see beyond the world, merely to see great mystery, what is plainly before my eyes ... With all respect to heaven the scene of miracle is here among us (Robinson, 2005b: 243)

Although Emerson's idiosyncratic idealism cannot comfortably be contained within the parameters of orthodox Christianity, Robinson herself has no problems affirming that this 'sweet man'[4] is articulating insights concerning the 'conversation that's gone on between humankind and the world since Genesis' (Robinson, in Schaub 1994: 249). Robinson is deeply immersed in the biblical narratives of creation and flood; exile and deliverance; baptism and regeneration. The Bible is another major resource which informs Robinson's use of water as a deep metaphor in *Housekeeping* and *Gilead*. The Genesis narratives have particularly powerful resonances for her. Feminist theologians have written about the submerged traces of the female chaos monster that inhabits the depths of the first creation narrative. They have also argued that the image of the Spirit of God brooding over the face of the waters offers support for reconciliation with the divine feminine that the monotheistic religions have banished from their sacred traditions.[5] Although *Housekeeping* was written when feminist theology was in its infancy, it is possible to argue that the ambivalent destructive and generative waters it describes are

---

[4]   See Schaub 1994: 240. Emerson's whole way of life as a poet/thinker, mystical theologian and abolitionist stands for Robinson as a unified whole exemplifying the integrative nature of his philosophy.

[5]   For an excellent discussion of such explorations in Genesis and their theological implications see Keller 2003.

similar to those portrayed in the first pages of the Bible. Interestingly Robinson's first non-fiction work, *Mother Country* (1989), is an impassioned indictment of the sin of polluting the seas. Here environmental concerns are heightened by her religious conviction that the oceans are the matrix of creation, and that it is not only a folly but also a blasphemy to pollute them. What is required, she has consistently argued, is a renewed sense of the sacredness of these waters to which their primacy in the biblical text alerts us.

This brief analysis of some of the sources that have contributed to Robinson's use of water as a deep metaphor provides the basis for my reading of *Housekeeping* and *Gilead*.

I have limited my focus to an investigation of Robinson's adaptation and use of resonant literary symbols rather than choosing another path and using psychoanalytic categories to mark a supposedly fluid female subjectivity in her writing. The latter approach has been fruitfully explored by a number of critics.[6] Their work raises important theological questions concerning female sacrality - but these are rather different from the ones that occupy me here.[7]

Life by drowning

The first pages of *Housekeeping* establish that this is a dangerous world. The firmament is thin, like sheet ice, and easily broken. The waters are dangerous and certainly will rise and overwhelm us.

The novel is set in the town of Fingerbone which is sited precariously on the shores of a deep lake. The water can show a calm countenance 'permeated by sunlight ... green life and innumerable fish' (1981: 9) but below the warm shallows lie the deeps; lightless and airless. 'At the foundation is the old lake, which is smothered and nameless and altogether black' (1981: 9).

> Sometimes in the spring this old lake will return. One will open a cellar door to waddling boots floating tallowy soles up and planks and buckets bumping at the threshold, the stairway gone from sight after the second step. The earth will brim, the soil will become mud and then silty water, and the grass will stand in chill water to its tips. (1981: 5)

Here we have a picture of the waters as a dark primeval power that has its own motion and cannot be prevented from welling up and flooding our human dwellings. This water also claims human lives. Ruthie, the

---

6   See, for example, Kaivola 1993; King 1996; Hedrick 1999.
7   I do discuss female subjectivity, the female imaginary and the female divine at length in *Literature, Theology and Feminism*, Walton 2007.

narrator, tells how her grandfather died as his train toppled spectacularly from the railway bridge and slid into the lake, 'like a weasel sliding off a rock' (1981: 6). The water absorbed this bulk 'becoming dull and opaque … By evening the lake … had sealed itself over' (1981: 8). Ruthie's mother, ominously married to a Mr Stone, also later sinks like one in these same depths.

These family tragedies, which shape Ruthie's life, are but particular instances of a universal fate. As Fingerbone discovers, after a particularly destructive flooding, the artefacts of civilization are like small charms and votive offerings utterly inadequate to appease an implacable deity. Memorials and tombstones are flattened, the library books are sodden, 'creating vast gaps in the Dewey system … Fungus and mold crept into wedding dresses and photograph albums' (1981: 62). And all of this is pre-ordained. God has sent a flood upon earth and even though the waters seem to have receded into small pools and ditches that appear to mirror heaven:

> One cannot cup one's hand and drink from the rim of any lake without remembering that mothers have died in it, lifting their children toward the air, though they must have known as they did so that the deluge would take all the children too. (1981: 193–4)

Passages like these seem to speak of blind and destructive forces indiscriminately obliterating human lives. Generation after generation are swept away. There is a truth in this view of existence; its bleakness resounds throughout the text. But it is only a partial truth. 'Curse and expel them … drown them in floods' (1981: 194) and the sorrow, the loss, the memories, the very absence of love people feel, become correspondingly strong and holy forces. So strong is our longing in the face of death that our loss pulls 'God Himself into the Vortex' (1981: 194). This earth-drawn God, Ruthie tells us, walks on water and does not drown (1981: 194). Ruthie senses there may be some way to embrace this elemental chaos that turns longing back into flesh (1981: 195). She dreams that her aunt Sylvie is teaching her to walk under water. This requires 'patience and grace, but she pulled me after her and our clothes flew like the robes of painted angels' (1981: 175).

Sylvie is a strange teacher and a very unlikely angel. She is a 'transient', a woman who recognizes the futility of housekeeping. Summoned home to care for her dead sister's children, she represents an altogether different approach to the encroaching waters than that taken by the citizens of Fingerbone. Happily she had chosen to marry a Fisher rather than a Stone[8]

---

[8]   As Robinson is not writing a realist novel she does not shrink from giving her characters names that correspond to their roles. Interestingly there is a third sister

(both husbands lend only their names to the narrative) and is someone who seems attuned to the fluidity of life and understands how to live upon the waters – although this form of existence, as Ruthie recognizes, is achingly uncomfortable and desperately insecure (1981: 83). Under her guardianship the girls find their family home is gradually transformed. Sylvie sleeps fully dressed, with her shoes beneath her pillow, as if outdoors and without shelter. She prefers the windows open and the lights switched off. Bats, swallows, leaves and insects, wind and rain begin to enter unopposed.

In a reflection upon mysticism Emerson wrote:

> The Eden of God is bare and grand: like the out-door landscape remembered from the evening fireside, it seems cold and desolate whilst you cower over the coals, but once abroad again, we pity those who can forego the magnificence of nature for candle light and cards. (1987 [1850]: 72)

A recurrent image in *Housekeeping* is that of observing a world of light and comfort from a place outside in the cold and darkness (1981: 54, 154, 203–4, 216–19). As her home undergoes a gradual transformation, Ruthie[9] is also being exiled from the mundane world and removed to another frightening realm 'outside'. For Robinson, as for Emerson, there is a correspondence between the natural landscape and the spiritual one. Ruthie is experiencing her own 'awakening'.[10] In a life marked by mourning and loss she has been progressively un-housed until 'neither threshold nor sill' (1981: 154) remain between her and a vision that could never be viewed in the warm glow of lamplight. Robinson's version of the magnificent 'Eden of God' is glimpsed by Ruthie when Sylvie bears her across the lake to a now deserted island. Ruthie views the ruins of dwellings and senses lost children, dead parents all around her. But in the place of desolation Sylvie has brought her to see, she also discovers a fantastic water garden. There is a 'flowering in the frost ... water drops spilled from all the trees as innumerably as petals' and trees 'fruit heavily

---

alongside Sylvie Fisher and Ruthie's mother, Helen Stone. Molly also becomes a fisher of sorts. She responds to an article in a missionary magazine entitled *I will make you fishers of men* and leaves Fingerbone for a life of exotic evangelism. Ruthie imagines this aunt to be engaged in some way in a work of cosmic redemption:

> Her net would sweep the turning world unremarked ... Such a net, such a harvesting would put an end to all anomaly. If it swept the whole floor of heaven it must finally sweep the black floor of Fingerbone too ... There would be a general reclaiming of fallen buttons and misplaced spectacles, of neighbors and kin, till time and error and accident were undone, and the world became comprehensible and whole. (1981: 91–2)

9   Her sister Lucille (whose name associates her with light) resists this relocation and migrates to the well-kept house of her domestic science teacher.

10   Interesting parallels can be drawn between Ruthie's path of withdrawal from conventional society and Edna's exclusion from her social world in Chopin's novel.

with bright globes of water' (1981: 152). She interprets her vision as confirming that need can blossom into everything it longs for. This is

> a foreshadowing – the world will be whole ... Lot's wife was salt and barren because she was full of loss and mourning and looked back. But here rare flowers would gleam in her hair, and on her breast, and in her hands, and there would be children all around her, to love and marvel at her for her beauty. (1981: 153)

It is Sylvie who makes possible Ruthie's vision and at this point in the narrative she is still dependent upon her aunt to survive upon the lake. In the final pages of the book Ruthie has a choice to make. Will she live in the 'outside world' as a sky-black-water-girl or go inside and be transformed 'by gross light into a mortal child' (1981: 204)? She chooses to follow Sylvie and leaves Fingerbone; walking out upon the water, perilously suspended above its dark surface, on the same bridge from which her grandfather fell. This is when she experiences her own epiphany and utter transformation:

> I believe it was the crossing of the bridge that changed me finally. The terrors of that crossing were considerable. Twice I stumbled and fell ...
> Something happened, something so memorable that when I think back to the crossing of that bridge, one moment bulges like the belly of a lens and all the others are at the peripheries and diminished. Was it only that the wind rose suddenly, so that we had to cower and lean against it like blind women groping their way along a wall? Or did we really hear some sound too loud to be heard, some word so true we did not understand it, but merely felt it pour through nerves like darkness or water? (1981: 215)

Like darkness or water.

A garden in Gilead

As many critics have argued, *Housekeeping* does not have a happy ending. Ruthie has followed Sylvie and can never now be like other people; the smell of lake water lingers where she passes (1981: 218). However, I have suggested that the water metaphor carries redemptive associations that are integrally associated with its darker meanings.[11] If the 'force behind the

---

[11]   My interpretation respects Robinson's claim to be 'Emersonian' (see Hedrick 1999: 137) but departs from the view that this entails a fatalistic acceptance of a ghastly fluidity in all things as Hedrick sometimes seems to imply:

> the essential miscibility of this world makes the notion of fixed boundaries, inside and outside, not just a laughable one for Emerson, but one that is morally

movement of time is a mourning that will not be comforted' this force is also our *only token* that there may be 'reconciliation and return ... there will be a garden' (1981: 192).

If *Housekeeping* is a book about dark waters the imagery in *Gilead* does at first appear to be altogether brighter. The book, set in Iowa in the 1950s, portrays human life as blessed by water. Some of the most delightful scenes take place in a garden that seems to be a domestic Eden – very different from the bare Eden of God! Here John Ames' seven-year-old son and his loved young wife play with water. They blow bubbles at the cat (2005a: 10) and spray each other with the hose: 'you two are dancing around in your iridescent little downpour, whooping and stomping as people ought to do when they encounter a thing as miraculous as water' (2005a: 72). Ames likens peace to 'a newly planted garden after warm rain' (2005a: 23) and witnesses the essence of joy as two lovers chase each other in a summer downpour:

> On some impulse, plain exuberance I suppose, the fellow jumped up and caught hold of a branch, and a storm of luminous water came pouring down on the two of them, and they laughed and took off running ... It was a beautiful thing to see. (2005a: 32)

When Ames first meets his wife she is drenched by rain (2005a: 184). Thereafter when he thinks of the gift she is to him he always remembers she came to him at Pentecost out of the rainstorm and that he baptized her with water, while marvelling at her beauty.

Ames, the clergyman, has an interesting perspective on baptism. He quotes Feuerbach: 'Water is the purest, clearest of liquids; in virtue of this, its natural character, it is the image of the spotless nature of the Divine Spirit ... there lies at the foundation of Baptism a beautiful, profound natural significance' (2005a: 27). Whilst baptism is 'a blessing' it 'does not enhance sacredness, but it acknowledges it' (2005a: 26). Here, in Emersonian fashion,[12] Ames recognizes the spiritual mysteries that flow

---

questionable. How can things change for the better, new ideas replace the old, wrongs be redressed if there is no such a thing as permanence. (Hedrick 1999: 143)

[12]   There are some sly references to Emerson's likeness to Ames in the biography Robinson gives her character. Like Emerson, Ames has a brother who studies at Göttingen and is turned away from faith by honest doubt. Like Emerson he also has a first wife who dies in her youth. In the image of an old man who has dared to fall in love we can hear echoes of Emerson in 'Circles':

> But the man and woman of seventy assume to know all, they have outlived their hope, they renounce aspiration, accept the actual for the necessary and talk down to the young. Let them then become organs of the Holy Ghost; let them be lovers; let them behold the truth; and their eyes are uplifted, their wrinkles smoothed, they are perfumed again with hope and power. (1979 [1841]: 189)

through our life in nature and are manifest in such elemental symbols. His ruminations on recognizing the sacredness of life lead him to recollect his childhood impulse to baptize some tiny kittens:

> I still remember how those warm little brows felt under the palm of my hand. Everyone has petted a cat, but to touch one like that with the pure intention of blessing it, is a very different thing ... The sensation of really knowing a creature, I mean really feeling its mysterious life and your own mysterious life at the same time. (2005a: 26)

As a grown man he has always loved to baptize people but wishes there were more 'shimmer and splash' in his tradition. He envies those pastors he has watched baptizing in the river: 'It was something to see the preacher lifting the one who was being baptized out of the water and the water pouring off the garments and the hair. It did look like a birth or a resurrection' (2005a: 72).

It is important that a minister understands how water heightens the touch of his blessing hand and knows the proper way to honour and to channel water. One of the funniest small incidents in the novel is the narrative of one of Ames' last pastoral duties. An old woman calls upon him for help when her world is turned upside down:

> She told me, considerably amazed that a reversal so drastic could occur in a lawful universe, that hot water came from the cold faucet and cold water from the hot faucet. I suggested she might just decide to take C for Hot and H for cold, but she said she liked things to work the way they were supposed to. So I came home and got my screw driver and came back and switched the handles ... Oh the clerical life! (2005a: 150)

Its touching descriptions of small events that mark the sanctity of everyday life are one reason why the book is held in such affection and why critics have been eager to append the word 'balm' to *Gilead* in their reviews – although Robinson herself resists this coupling. In fact the novel has a much darker subtext. It is not only the story of an elderly clergyman who has come very late to love and fatherhood; it is also the story of lost loves and lost children, lost vision.

Hélène Cixous argues that whenever we really love, death enters our lives and begins to strip us bare: 'as soon as I love death is there, it camps right out in the middle of my body, getting mixed up with my food' (1998: 86). Ames affirms this poignancy. He becomes aware of his mortality at precisely the point where he allows himself to fall in love. He knows he is old and dying and that the ecstasy of his rain-fresh Eden is but for a moment. This is a torment. Love for Ames is 'a foretaste of death, at least of dying. Anyway why should that seem strange? "Passion" is the word we use after all' (2005a: 233).

In perhaps the most painful water scene in the text Ames describes a baby playing with its mother in the water:

> The baby cupped her hands and poured water on her mother's arm and laughed, so her mother cupped her hands and poured water on the baby's belly. And the baby laughed ... The baby made a conversational sound and her mother said, 'That's a leaf. A leaf off a tree. Leaf,' and gave it into the baby's hand. And the sun was shining as well as it could onto that shadowing river ... And the cicadas were chanting, and the willows were straggling their tresses in the water. (2005a: 186-7)

Even as they enjoy this narrative of primordial innocence, readers are already aware that this water baby has long ago died of poverty, neglect and cruelty. No wonder Ames remarked about this scene still vivid in his memory, 'I do not understand one thing in this world. Not one' (2005a: 187).

Similarly, although baptism is a recurring theme in the text it is also an ambivalent one. Alongside Ames' reflections upon its sacredness stand the stories of two 'failed' baptisms. Ames lost his first wife in childbirth and his infant daughter died shortly later. Because the labour was early, and he was away from home at the time, his best friend and clergy colleague, Broughton, baptized the girl and gave her the name Angeline. Ames resents this. He had already chosen his daughter's name. She was to be Rebecca, the woman who drew water from the well (Genesis 24), not an angel. Fifty years later Ames still struggles with this misnaming. The second error is more tragic. Because Broughton believed his friend Ames would never now have a child he asked him to baptize his own son and then surprised him by announcing during the service that the boy would be called John Ames Broughton. Ames' grief is such that he cannot accept this gift of love. The man who felt the tender and mysterious life of tiny kittens does not bless this little child:

> As it was, my heart froze in me and I thought, This is *not* my child – which I truly had not thought of any child before ...
>
> I have thought from time to time that the child felt how coldly I went about its christening, how far my thoughts were from blessing him ... And I do feel a burden of guilt towards that child ...
>
> I do wish I could christen him again ... I did not feel the sacredness under my hand that I always do feel. (2005a: 214)

Ames' namesake, his 'elder son', leads a wandering and blighted life and Ames always feels responsible for withholding his birthright.

When we consider passages such as these we begin to realize Ames' world is neither calm nor bright nor innocent. What is true for him is also true for the town he has served throughout his ministry. Gilead was

established as an outpost of freedom, a refuge for escaping slaves. It
endured the desperate violence of the civil war and its people (including
Ames' grandfather – a soldier pastor) committed the usual crimes of war
in their struggle for freedom. Whilst not cleansed from these atrocities it
is forgetful of its radical past. Gilead is marred by racism and unable to
provide refuge for John Ames Broughton's black wife and child. As a
writer deeply steeped in the Bible, Robinson is aware that Gilead is an
ambiguous place to live:

> The biblical Gilead has a very complex history. It's a town that's criticized
> for being rich and hard-hearted; it's also lamented because it's been
> destroyed; and it's also used as a symbol of what can be restored, what can
> be hoped for. I like the name because of its various associations and
> meanings. (Robinson, in Rothenburg: 2004)

A third ambivalent baptism should be mentioned in relation to the town.
Towards the end of the novel Ames dreams that he and Broughton are
boys again playing in the river. His grandfather, who represents both the
violent and prophetic radicalism of Gilead's past,

> stalked out of the trees in that furious way he had, scooped his hat full of
> water and threw it over us, billowing in the air like a veil, and fell down
> over us. Then he put his hat on his head and stalked off into the trees again
> and left us standing there in that glistening river, amazed at ourselves and
> shining like the apostles. (2005a: 231)

This event Ames interprets as his grandfather throwing his mantle over
him and he wonders whether his earthly loves – 'I was reflecting on that
day I first saw your mother, that blessed rainy, Pentecost' (2005a: 231)
– may have somehow weakened his zealous faith. Has he failed Gilead?
Has the town become a place of dust and ashes as his grandfather proph-
esied? He comes to believe not and to claim the passion which inspired
the saints and martyrs in their prodigal renunciations could also be made
manifest in ordinary, imperfect mortal loves (2005a: 232) and in weak
and weary places like Gilead.

Does this novel have a happy ending? Ames gets to bless his namesake
at last but recognizes that his godson's black family will never be welcome
in Gilead. He knows the town has not become the 'bold ramparts meant
to shelter … peace' (2005a: 277) it was founded to be. Nevertheless, he
can imagine giving his body to Gilead in death as a kind of last wild act
of love that entails an embrace of the mortal life he has lived, the place
he has inhabited and the losses he has endured. All soon to be swept away
but all touched by grace (2005a: 282).

Wide waters

When I think of the ways Robinson has used water imagery in her two novels I imagine a world that is built on a wide stretch of water.

At the far side of this the deeps are savage and unpredictable. There are no houses on the banks, no jetties, harbours or quays. A few lost and frightened people seek shelter on the thin rim of the shore but the only way of escape lies through the wild water and the only way to survive is to have the sea in your veins. No choice but to abandon yourself to the floods. Few are brave enough to do this and time after time the small driftwood vessels in which they seek to ride the waves are wrecked upon the rocks. But here a mystery occurs. In the boiling seas are sweet currents that can scoop the exhausted swimmers from the seabed, raise them again to the air and carry them to calmer places. Sometimes even the foolish sailors are accidentally caught in these fresh water streams; but only when their boats are gone and they have tasted drowning.

On the near side of the water there is a thriving settlement. People have built homes and they tend fields and gardens. These reach right to the water's edge and the carrots and cabbages they pull up for supper have sand in their roots. No one is fearful of making a day trip on a pleasure boat and the fishing vessels bring home fine catches of slim silver fish – and an occasional dark warty monster from the deep. But the people who live in this town, although they appear to be happy and content, spend the long summer evenings looking out to sea. In winter they risk high tides to walk along the shore. Sooner or later most are compelled to voyage out. Children stow away on ships. Betrayed lovers walk out fully clothed into the sea at midnight. Young men buy compasses and telescopes and old men pore over charts and maps. Women dress as sailors and sign ship's papers. They abandon their families for crusades or pilgrimages. The smoke continues to rise from the chimneys and the gardens produce their fruit and flowers but the people always venture out at last into the turbulent deep.

The point is, of course, that this is the same wide stretch of water. It only appears to us to be different according to how we experience it. The waters of God are violent and dark. They are also gentle and calm. If we find life here we also find death and never the one without the other. Questioned about differing use of water in both novels, Robinson acknowledges that although the books appear very different there is this underlying connection between them. She describes this in terms of her theological understanding of Christian baptism:

> Well, they're very different books, of course. But I think one of the things that's very striking about baptism as an idea, in terms of the language with which it's dealt with biblically, is that it's a baptism into death ... So the idea of blessing and the fact of mortality are very implicit together. (Owens: 2007)

Elsewhere Robinson affirms that a biblical perspective can be traced in her earlier work and argues that Ruthie has taken an ancient religious path, that of renunciation, in order to experience reconciliation: 'It's what every prophet in the Bible does' (Robinson, in Schaub 1994: 243).

Because Robinson emphatically claims the significance of biblical themes within each novel, it does not mean that we should deny the dark and tragic elements that pervade each text. Orthodox believers find comfort in their scriptures but Robinson, who has attended church and read the Bible all her life, says that she finds the message it communicates disturbing, alien and painful: 'What can these strange stories mean? After so much time and event and so much revelation, the mystery is only confounded' (2005b: 243). Reflecting further upon the Bible, Robinson, like Ames, connects the meaning of its holy symbols with our passionate loves for the world in its motion, substance and imperfect glory. The text does not contain the truth of our experience; it heightens or illuminates it. It is in living that we encounter the terror and tenderness of God. Scripture and theology come later and are secondary. Literature, in its scrupulous attention to experience, may sometimes draw closer to sacred truth. However, we must always discern a 'profounder intuition than language does justice to' and distinguish 'between the traces that religion leaves on the text, and the thing itself' (Robinson, in Montgomery-Fate 2006: 42).[13]

In this frame it is possible to affirm the redemptive biblical motifs which are to be found in the water symbolism of both *Housekeeping* and *Gilead*, but to receive these anew as traces of ecstasy and terror similar to those encountered in Emerson, Melville and Chopin and, indeed, in our everyday existence. Robinson offers a parable which I find helpful in comprehending the way we encounter the sacred in her work. She takes the biblical image of the seed that must die in order to bear fruit. God's pattern is coded in the husk but this can only come to fruition as it is embraced by the earth and awoken to blossoming by water:

> John Calvin says when a seed falls in to the ground it is cherished there
> ... One might as well say the earth invades the seed, seizes it as occasion
> to compose itself in some brief shape. Groundwater in a sleeve of tissue,

---

13   Robinson states:

   I'm increasingly aware that I am the inheritor of a particular theological tradition, which comes from John Calvin. Calvinism is based on the idea that experience itself has a revelatory quality, and that the mind is the locus of revelation, since it is the mind of the perceiver. Experience can draw one forward in terms of comprehension, in terms of what one is given to know. It's the idea that God is living, and in continuous conversation with you. You're always instructed anew in ways that will disturb what you experienced before. An open theology then is one where you feel you're being led through the experience of life in order to have a profounder understanding. (in Montgomery-Fate 2006: 39) flaunting improbable fragrances and iridescences as the things of this strange world are inclined to do ... teasing hope beyond itself ... a parable brilliant with strangeness, cryptic with wisdom, disturbing as a tender intention full of ... frightening mercy. (2005b: 234)

Bibliography

Adams, Richard (1974), *Watership Down* (Harmondsworth: Penguin).

Adorno, Theodor (2000), 'Commitment', in A. Arato and E. Gebhardt (eds), *The Essential Frankfurt School Reader* (New York: Continuum): 300–18.

Allen, Judith and Sally Kitch (1998), 'Disciplined by Disciplines? The Need for an Interdisciplinary Research Mission in Women's Studies', *Feminist Studies* 24.2: 275–99.

Alves, Rubem (1990), *The Poet, the Warrior, the Prophet* (London: SCM Press).

Antze, Paul and Michael Lambek (1996b), 'Introduction: Forecasting Memory', in P. Antze and M. Lambek (eds), *Tense Past: Cultural Essays in Trauma and Memory* (London: Routledge): xi–xxxviii.

Anzaldúa, Gloria (1993), 'La conciencia de la mestiza: Towards a new consciousness', in Linda S. Kauffman (ed.), *American Feminist Thought at Century's End* (Cambridge, MA: Blackwell): 427–40.

Auerbach, Erich (1953), *Mimesis: The Representation of Reality in Western Literature* (Princeton: Princeton University Press).

Balsamo, Anne (1999), 'Reading Cyborgs Writing Feminism', in Wolmark 1999: 145–56.

Bhabha, Homi K. (1994), *The Location of Culture* (London: Routledge).

Blanchot, Maurice (1995), *The Writing of the Disaster*, tr. A. Smock (Lincoln: University of Nebraska Press).

Braidotti, Rosi (1991), *Patterns of Dissonance: A Study of Women in Contemporary Society* (Cambridge: Polity).

—— (1994), *Nomadic Subjects: Embodiment and Sexual Difference in Contemporary Feminist Thought* (New York: Columbia University Press).

Brock, Rita Nakashima (1988), *Journeys by Heart: A Christology of Erotic Power* (New York: Crossroad).

—— (1993), 'Dusting the Bible on the Floor', in E. Fiorenza (ed.), *Searching the Scriptures*, Vol. 1 (London: SCM Press): 64–75.

Brown, Delwin, S. G. Davaney and K. Tanner (eds) (2001*), Converging on Culture: Theologians in Dialogue with Cultural Analysis and Criticism* (Oxford: Oxford University Press).

Buker, Eloise (2003), 'Is Women's Studies a Disciplinary or an Interdisciplinary Field of Inquiry?', *National Women's Studies Association Journal*, Vol. 15, no. 1., Spring, pp. 73–93.

Butler, Judith (1990), *Gender Trouble and the Subversion of Identity* (London: Routledge).

Butler, Judith, John Guillory and Kendall Thomas (eds) (2000), *What's Left of Theory: New Work on the Politics of Literary Theory* (London: Routledge).

Cannon, Katie (1988), *Black Womanist Ethics* (Atlanta: Scholars Press).

Caputo, John (1993), *Against Ethics* (Bloomington: Indiana University Press).

—— (2006), *The Weakness of God: A Theology of the Event* (Bloomington: Indiana University Press).

Celan, Paul (1978 [1960]), 'The Meridian', *The Chicago Review* 29.3: 29–40.

Chopin, Kate (1988 [1899]), *The Awakening* (New York: Bantam Classics).

Chopp, Rebecca (1991), *The Power to Speak: Feminism, Language, God* (New York: Crossroad).

—— (1995), *Saving Work: Feminist Practices of Theological Education* (Louisville: Westminster/John Knox Press).

—— (2001), 'Theology and the Poetics of Testimony', in D. Brown, S. G. Davaney and K. Tanner 2001: 56–70.

Christ, Carol (1979 [1975]), 'Spiritual Quest and Women's Experience', in Christ and Plaskow 1979: 228–45.

—— (1980), *Diving Deep and Surfacing: Women Writers on the Spiritual Quest* (Boston: Beacon Press).

Christ, Carol and Judith Plaskow (eds) (1979), *Womanspirit Rising: A Feminist Reader in Religion* (San Francisco: Harper & Row).

—— (1979a), 'Preface', in Christ and Plaskow 1979: ix–xi.

—— (1979b), 'Introduction', in Christ and Plaskow 1979: 1–18.

—— (1989), *Weaving the Visions: New Patterns in Feminist Spirituality* (New York: HarperCollins).

—— (1989), 'Introduction', in Christ and Plaskow 1989: 1–14.

Cixous, Hélène (1979), *Vivre l'Orange/To Live the Orange* (Paris: des femmes).

—— (1982), *Limonade tout baid si infini* (Paris: des femmes).

—— (1988), 'Extreme Fidelity', tr. A. Liddle and S. Sellers, in S. Sellers (ed.), *Writing Differences: Readings from the Seminars of Hélène Cixous* (Milton Keynes: Open University Press, 9–35).

—— (1989 [1975]), 'Sorties: Out and Out: Attacks/Ways Out/Forays', tr. A. Liddle, in C. Belsey and J. Moore (eds), *The Feminist Reader* (London: Macmillan): 101–16.

—— (1990 [1975]), 'The Laugh of the Medusa', in D. Walder (ed.), *Literature in the Modern World* (Oxford: Oxford University Press).

—— (1993), *Three Steps on the Ladder of Writing*, tr. S. Cornell and S. Sellers (New York: Columbia University Press).

—— (1994a), *The Cixous Reader*, Susan Sellers (ed.) (London: Routledge).

—— (1994b), *Manna to the Mandelstams to the Mandelas*, tr. Catherine MacGillivray (Minneapolis: University of Minnesota Press).

—— (1998), *Stigmata: Escaping Texts* (London: Routledge).

Cixous, Hélène and Mirielle Gruber (1997), *Hélène Cixous Rootprints: Memory and Life Writing* (London: Routledge).

Clack, Beverley (2005), 'Shaping Feminist Theology: A Pragmatic Approach?', *Feminist Theology* 13.2: 249–64.

Crites, Stephen (1997 [1971]), 'The Narrative Quality of Experience', in Hauerwas and Jones 1997: 65–88.

Crossan, John D. (1975), *The Dark Interval: Towards a Theology of Story* (Niles: Argus).

Culler, Johnathan (2000), 'The Literary in Theory', in Butler, Guillory and Kendall 2000: 273–92.

Cupitt, Don (1991), *What is a Story?* (London: SCM Press).

Curti, Linda (1998), *Female Stories, Female Bodies* (Basingstoke: Macmillan).

Daly, Mary (1984), *Pure Lust: Elemental Feminist Philosophy* (London: Women's Press).

De Lauretis, Teresa (1987), *Technologies of Gender: Essays on Theory, Film and Fiction* (London: Macmillan).

Durber, Susan (2007), 'A Pulpit Princess? Preaching Like a Woman', *Theology and Sexuality* 13.2: 167–74.

Eaglestone, Robert (1997), *Ethical Criticism: Reading After Levinas* (Edinburgh: Edinburgh University Press).

Eagleton, Terry (2004), *After Theory* (London: Penguin).

Eliot, T. S. (1939), *The Idea of a Christian Society* (London: Faber & Faber).

—— (1951 [1935]), 'Religion and Literature', in *Selected Essays* (London: Faber & Faber): 388–401.

Emerson, Ralph Waldo (1979 [1841]), 'Circles', in Joseph Slater, Alfred Ferguson and Jean Carr (eds), *The Collected Works of Ralph Waldo Emerson*, Vol. 2 (Cambridge, MA: Harvard University Press): 177–90.

—— (1987 [1850]), 'Swedenborg, or the Mystic', in Joseph Slater and Douglas Wilson (eds), *The Collected Works of Ralph Waldo Emerson*, Vol. 4 (Cambridge, MA: Harvard University Press): 51–82.

Felman, Shoshona (1992a), 'Education and Crisis, or the Vicissitudes of Teaching', in Felman and Laub 1992: 1–56.

—— (1992b), 'After the Apocalypse: Paul de Man and the Fall to Silence', in Felman and Laub 1992: 120–64.

Felman, Shoshona and D. Laub (eds) (1992), *Testimony: Crises of Witnessing in Literature, Psychoanalysis and History* (London: Routledge).

Fiddes, Paul (1991), *Freedom and Limit: A Dialogue between Literature and Christian Doctrine* (Houndmills: Macmillan).

Fiorenza, Elisabeth Schussler (1983), *In Memory of Her: A Feminist Theological Reconstruction of Christian Origins* (London: SCM Press).

——— (1995), *Jesus, Miriam's Child, Sophia's Prophet: Critical Issues in Feminist Christology* (London: SCM Press).

Ford, David (1981), *Barth and God's Story* (Frankfurt: Verlag Peter Lang).

Foucault, Michel (1994), *The Order of Things: Archaeology of the Human Sciences* (New York: Vintage Books).

——— (2002), *Archaeology of Knowledge*, tr. Sheridan Smith (London: Routledge).

Frei, Hans (1974), *The Eclipse of Biblical Narrative: A Study in Eighteenth and Nineteenth Century Hermeneutics* (New Haven: Yale University Press).

——— (1993), *Theology and Narrative: Selected Essays* (Oxford: Oxford University Press).

Friedman, Susan Stanford (1998), '(Inter)Disciplinarity and the Question of the Woman's Studies PhD', *Feminist Studies* 24.3: 301–25.

Fulkerson, Mary McClintock (1994), *Changing the Subject: Women's Discourses and Feminist Theology* (Minneapolis: Fortress Press).

Goldberg, Michael (1991), *Theology and Narrative: A Critical Introduction* (Philadelphia: Trinity Press International).

Graham, Elaine (1995), *Making the Difference: Gender, Personhood and Theology* (London: Mowbray).

——— (2002), *Representations of the Post/human: Monsters, Aliens and Others in Popular Culture* (Manchester: Manchester University Press).

Greene, Gayle (1991), *Changing the Story: Feminist Fiction and the Tradition* (Chicago: University of Chicago Press).

Greene, Graham (1955), *The Quiet American* (London: Heinemann).

Greer, Germaine (1993 [1971]), *The Female Eunuch* (London: HarperCollins).

Greiner, Donald (1993), *Women without Men: Female Bonding and the American Novel of the 1980s* (Columbia, South Carolina: University of South Carolina Press).

Grey, Mary (2003), *Sacred Longings: Ecofeminist Theology and Globalisation* (London: SCM Press).

Haraway, Donna (1991a), 'Situated Knowledge: The Science Question in Feminism and the Privilege of Partial Perspective', in D. Haraway, *Simians, Cyborgs and Women* (London: Free Association Books).

—— (1991b), 'A Cyborg Manifesto: Science, Technology and Socialist-Feminism in the Late Twentieth Century', in D. Haraway, *Simians, Cyborgs and Women* (London: Free Association Books).

Harding, Sandra (1991), *Whose Science? Whose Knowledge? Thinking from Women's Lives* (Ithaca, NY: Cornell University Press).

Hauerwas, Stanley (1981), *A Community of Character: Toward a Constructive Christian Ethic* (Notre Dame: University of Notre Dame Press).

—— (1994), *Dispatches from the Front: Theological Engagements with the Secular* (Durham and London: Duke University Press).

Hauerwas, Stanley and L. Gregory Jones (eds) (1997), *Why Narrative: Readings in Narrative Theology* (Eugene, OR: Wipf and Stock Publishers).

HD (1983), 'Trilogy', in *HD: Collected Poems* (New York: New Direction Books): 505–612.

Hedrick, Tace (1999), '"The Perimeters of Our Wandering are Nowhere": Breaching the Domestic in *Housekeeping*', *Critique', Studies in Contemporary Fiction* 40.2: 137–51.

Hillesum, Etty (1999 [1981] *An Interrupted Life: The Diaries and Letters of Etty Hillesum*, tr. Arnold Pomerans (London: Persephone Books).

Hodgson, Peter (2001), *Theology in the Fiction of George Eliot* (London: SCM Press).

Hoffman, Eva (1999 [1996]), 'Introduction', in Etty Hillesum, *An Interrupted Life: The Diaries and Letters of Etty Hillesum*, tr. Arnold Pomerans (London: Persephone Books).

Humm, Maggie (1994), *A Reader's Guide to Contemporary Feminist Literary Criticism* (London: Harvester Wheatsheaf).

Irigaray, Luce (1985), *Speculum of the Other Woman*, tr. Catherine Porter (Ithaca, NY: Cornell University Press).

—— (1991), *Marine Lover of Friedrich Nietzsche*, tr. G. Gill (New York: Columbia University Press).

—— (1993a), *Sexes and Genealogies*, tr. Gillian Gill (New York: Columbia University Press).

—— (1993b), *je, tu, nous: Towards a Culture of Difference*, tr. Alison Martin (London: Routledge).

—— (1993c), *An Ethics of Sexual Difference*, tr. G. Gill (London: Athlone Press).

Jardine, Alice (1985), *Gynesis: Configurations of Women and Modernity* (Ithaca, NY: Cornell University Press).

Jasper, David (1987), 'The Limits of Formalism and the Theology of Hope: Ricoeur, Moltmann and Dostoevsky', *Literature and Theology* 1.1: 1–10.

—— (1992), 'The Study of Literature and Theology: Five Years On', *Literature and Theology* 6.1: 1–10.

—— (1993), *Rhetoric, Power and Community: An Exercise in Reserve* (London: Macmillan).

Jasper, David, Nicholas Sagovsky, Michael Wheeler, Terry Wright, Alison Milbank and John Milbank (1987), 'Editorial', *Literature and Theology* 1.1: iii-v.

Kaivola, Karen (1993), 'The Pleasures and Perils of Merging: Female Subjectivity in Marilynne Robinson's *Housekeeping*', *Contemporary Literature* 34.4: 670–90.

Kant, Immanuel ([1798] 1979), *The Conflict of the Faculties*, tr. Mary J. Gregor (New York: Arabis).

Kaufman, Gordon (1993a), *In the Face of a Mystery: A Constructive Theology* (Cambridge, MA: Harvard University Press).

—— (1993b), 'Reconstructing the Concept of God', in S. Coakley and D. Pailin (eds), *The Making and Remaking of Christian Doctrine: Essays in Honour of Maurice Wiles* (Oxford: Clarendon Press): 95–115.

—— (1995), *An Essay on Theological Method* (Atlanta: Scholars Press).

Kearney, Richard (2004), *On Paul Ricoeur: The Owl of Minerva* (Aldershot: Ashgate).

Keller, Katherine (2003), *Face of the Deep: A Theology of Becoming* (London: Routledge).

King, Kirstin (1996), 'Resurfacing of the Deeps: Semiotic Balance in Marilynne Robinson's *Housekeeping*', *Studies in the Novel* 28.4: 565–81.

Klein, Julie Thompson (1990), *Interdisciplinarity: History, Theory and Practice* (Detroit: Wayne State University Press).

Kojecky, Roger (1971), *T. S. Eliot's Social Criticism* (London: Faber & Faber).

Kristeva, Julia (1980), *Desire in Language: A Semiotic Approach to Literature and Art* (Oxford: Blackwell).

—— (1982), *Powers of Horror: An Essay on Abjection*, tr. Leon Roudiez (New York: Columbia University Press).

—— (2000), *The Sense and Non-sense of Revolt*, tr. Jeanine Herman (New York: Columbia University Press).

Kroker, Arthur (1980), 'Migration across the Disciplines', *Journal of Canadian Studies* 15: 3–10.

Krondorfer, Bjorn H. (2007), 'Who's Afraid of Gay Theology?', *Theology and Sexuality* 13.3:257–74.

Lauret, Maria (1994), *Liberating Literature: Feminist Fiction in America* (London: Routledge).

Le Doeuff, Michèle (2002 [1980]), *The Philosophical Imaginary*, tr. C. Gordon (London: Continuum).

Ledbetter, Mark (1997), 'Centre Shouts and Peripheral Echoes', in K. Tsuchiya (ed.), *Dissent and Marginality: Essays on the Border of Literature and Religion* (Basingstoke: Macmillan): 115–25.

Lessing, Doris (1973), *The Golden Notebook* (London: Grafton Books).

Lindbeck, George (1984), *The Nature of Doctrine: Religion and Theology in a Postliberal Age* (Philadelphia: Westminster Press).

Long, Asphodel (1992), *In a Chariot Drawn by Lions* (London: The Women's Press).

Loughlin, Gerard (1996), *Telling God's Story: Bible, Church and Narrative Theology* (Cambridge: Cambridge University Press).

Lucy, Sean (1960), *T. S. Eliot and the Idea of Tradition* (London: Cohen and West).

Lyotard, Jean-François (1988), 'Can Thought Go On Without a Body?', *Discourse* 11.1: 74–87.

MacGillivray, Catherine (1994), 'The Political IS – (and the) Poetical', in H. Cixous 1994b: xii–xlix (xlix).

MacIntyre, Alasdair (1981), *After Virtue: A Study in Moral Theory* (London: Duckworth).

McFague, Sallie (1993), *The Body of God: An Ecological Theology* (London: SCM Press).

McIntosh, Mark (1998), *Mystical Theology: The Integrity of Spirituality and Theology* (Oxford: Blackwell).

McNay, Lois (2000), *Gender and Agency* (Cambridge: Polity Press).

Moi, Toril (2003), 'Feminist Theory After Theory', in Michael Payne and John Schad (eds), *life.after.theory* (London: Continuum): 133–67.

Montgomery-Fate, Tom (2006), 'Seeing the Holy: Marilynne Robinson Explores the Sacredness of the Everyday World', *Sojourners* 35.6: 38–43.

Morrison, Toni (1987), *Beloved* (London: Chatto & Windus).

Newlands, George (2004), *The Transformative Imagination* (Aldershot: Ashgate).

Nixon, Nicola (1999), 'Cyberpunk: Preparing the Ground for Revolution or Keeping the Boys Satisfied', in Wolmark 1999: 191–207.

Nussbaum, Martha (1986), *The Fragility of Goodness: Luck and Ethics in Greek Tragedy* (Cambridge: Cambridge University Press).

—— (1990), *Love's Knowledge: Essays on Philosophy and Literature* (Oxford: Oxford University Press).

—— (1997), 'Narrative Emotions: Beckett's Genealogy of Love', in Hauerwas and Jones 1997: 216–50.

Ostriker, Alicia (1993), *Feminist Revision and the Bible* (Oxford, Blackwell).

—— (1997), *The Nakedness of the Fathers: Biblical Visions and Revisions* (New Brunswick: Rutgers University Press).

Owens, Jill (2007), 'The Epistolary Marilynne Robinson', http://www.powells.com/authors/robinson.html (accessed 10 February 2007).

Pacini, David (1994), 'Symbol Then and Now: Remembering and Connecting', in David Jasper and Mark Ledbetter (eds), *In Good Company: Essays in Honour of Robert Detweiler* (Atlanta: Scholars Press): 121–50.

Pagels, Elaine (1988), *Adam, Eve and the Serpent* (London: Weidenfeld & Nicolson).

Parsons, Susan, ed. (2002), *The Cambridge Companion to Feminist Theology* (Cambridge: Cambridge University Press).

Parsons, Susan (2002a), 'Preface', in Parsons 2002: xiii–xvii.

—— (2002b), 'Feminist Theology as Dogmatic Theology', in Parsons 2002: 114–34.

Plantinga, Alvin (1974), *God, Freedom, and Evil* (Grand Rapids, MI: William B. Eerdmans).

Plaskow, Judith (1980), *Sex, Sin and Grace: Women's Experience and the Theologies of Reinhold Niebuhr and Paul Tillich* (Washington: University Press of America).

—— (1989), 'Jewish Memory in Feminist Perspective', in Christ and Plaskow (eds), *Weaving the Visions*, 39–50.

—— (1990), *Standing Again at Sinai* (San Francisco: Harper and Row).

Procter-Smith, Marjorie (1998), '"Reorganising Victimisation": The Intersection between Liturgy and Domestic Violence', in C. Adams and M. Fortune (eds), *Violence Against Women and Children: A Theological Source Book* (New York: Continuum): 428–43.

Prosser, Diane (1995), *Transgressive Corporeality: The Body, Poststructuralism and the Theological Imagination* (New York: SUNY Press).

Pryse, Marjorie (1998), 'Critical Interdisciplinarity, Women's Studies, and Cross-Cultural Insight', *NWSA Journal* 10.1: 1–22.

Raschke, Carl (1988), *Theological Thinking: An Inquiry* (Atlanta: Scholars Press).

Reuther, Rosemary (1983), *Sexism and God Talk* (London: SCM Press).

Rich, Adrienne (1978a), *The Dream of a Common Language* (New York: W. W. Norton).

—— (1978b), 'When We Dead Awaken: Writing as Re-vision', in Adrienne Rich, *On Lies, Secrets and Silences: Selected Prose 1966–1978* (New York: W. W. Norton).

Ricoeur, Paul (1985), *Time and Narrative, Volume Two* (Chicago: University of Chicago Press).

—— (1991), *A Ricoeur Reader: Reflection and Imagination*, ed. Mario Valde (Hemel Hempstead: Harvester Wheatsheaf).

Roberts, Michèle (1983), 'The Woman Who Wanted to Be a Hero', in J. Garcia and S. Maitland (eds), *Walking on the Water: Women Talk About Spirituality* (London: Virago): 50–65.

—— (1991[1984]), *The Wild Girl* (London: Minerva).

—— (1992), *Daughters of the House* (London: Virago).

—— (1995), 'Restoration Work in Palazzo Te', in M. Roberts, *All the Selves I Was* (London: Virago): 57–8.

—— (1998), *Impossible Saints* (London: Virago).

Robinson, Marilynne (1981), *Housekeeping* (London: Faber & Faber).

—— (1988), "Introduction", in Kate Chopin, *The Awakening* (New York: Bantam Classics): vii–xxii.

—— (1989), *Mother Country: Britain, the Welfare State and Nuclear Pollution* (New York, Farrar).

—— (2005a), *Gilead* (London: Virago).

—— (2005b [1998]), *The Death of Adam: Essays on Modern Thought* (New York: Picador).

Roemer, Michael (1995), *Postmodernism and the Invalidation of Traditional Narrative* (Lanham, MD: Rowman and Littlefield).

Rothenburg, Jennie (2004), 'Gilead's Balm', http://www.theatlantic.com/doc/200411u/int2004-11-17 (accessed 10 February 2007).

Ryan, Katy (2005), 'Horizons of Grace', *Philosophy and Literature* 29: 349–64.

Saiving, Valerie (1979 [1960]), 'The Human Situation: A Feminine View', in Christ and Plaskow 1979: 25–42.

Sands, Kathleen (1994), *Escape from Paradise: Evil and Tragedy in Feminist Theology* (Minneapolis: Fortress Press).

Schaub, Thomas (1994), 'An Interview with Marilynne Robinson', *Contemporary Literature* 35.2: 232–51.

Shange, Ntozake (1986 [1975]), *For colored girls who have considered suicide / when the rainbow is enuf* (New York: Bantam Books).

Showalter, Elaine (1979), *A Literature of Their Own: From Charlotte Brontë to Doris Lessing* (London: The Women's Press).

—— (1986a), *The New Feminist Criticism: Essays on Women, Literature and Theory* (London: Virago).

—— (1986b), 'Feminist Criticism in the Wilderness', in Showalter 1986a: 243 –70.

Smart, Elizabeth (1992a [1945]), *By Grand Central Station I Sat Down and Wept* (London: Flamingo).

—— (1992b), *Necessary Secrets: The First Volume of Elizabeth Smart's Journals*, ed. A. Van Wart (London: Paladin).

———— (1992c), *The Collected Poems* (London: Paladin).

Soussioff, Catherine and Marc Franco (2002), 'Visual and Performance Studies: A New History of Interdisciplinarity', *Social Text* 20.4: 29–46.

Sullivan, Rosemary (1992), *By Heart: The Life of Elizabeth Smart* (London: Flamingo).

Taylor, Charles (2004), *Modern Social Imaginaries* (Durham and London: Duke University Press).

Taylor, Mark C. (1984), *Erring: A Postmodern A/theology* (Chicago: University of Chicago Press).

Thistlethwaite, Susan (1989), *Sex, Race and God: Christian Feminism in Black and White* (London: Geoffrey Chapman).

Tracy, David (1981), *The Analogical Imagination* (London: SCM Press).

Trible, Phyllis (1992), Texts of Terror: Literary-Feminist Readings of Biblical Narratives (London: SCM Press).

Valdes, Mario (1991), 'Introduction', in M. Valdes (ed.), *A Ricoeur Reader: Reflection and Imagination* (Hemel Hempstead: Harvester Wheatsheaf).

van Heijst, Annelies (1995), *Longing for the Fall* (Kampen: Kok Pharos Publishing House).

———— (2007), *Literature, Theology and Feminism* (Manchester: Manchester University Press).

Walker, Alice (1983), *The Color Purple* (London: The Women's Press).

———— (1984), *In Search of Our Mother's Gardens: Womanist Prose* (London: The Women's Press).

Walton, Heather (1999), 'Passion and Pain: Conceiving Theology Out of Infertility', *Contact: The Interdisciplinary Journal of Pastoral Studies* 130: 3–9.

———— (2003), 'Advent: Theological Reflections on IVF', *Theology and Sexuality* 9.2: 201–9.

———— (2007), *Literature, Theology and Feminism* (Manchester: Manchester University Press).

Walton, Heather and Susan Durber (1994), *Silence in Heaven: A Book of Women's Preaching* (London: SCM Press).

Ward, G. (2005), 'Postmodern Theology', in David Ford (ed.), *The Modern Theologians* (Oxford: Blackwell): 322–38.

Webster, Dan (2003), 'Marilynne Robinson', http://www.spokesman review.com/interactive/bookclub/interviews/interview.asp?IntID=5 (accessed 10 February 2007).

Weedon, Chris (1987), *Feminist Practice and Poststructuralist Theory* (Oxford: Blackwell).

Williams, Rowan (1986), 'On Ricoeur', *Modern Theology* 2.3: 197–211.

Winquist, Charles (1995), *Desiring Theology* (Chicago: University of Chicago Press).

Wolmark, Jenny (ed.) (1999), *Cybersexualities: A Reader on Feminist Theory, Cyborgs and Cyberspace* (Edinburgh: Edinburgh University Press).

—— (1999a), 'Cybersexualities: Cyborgs and Cyberpunks', in Wolmark 1999: 137–9.

—— (1999b), 'The Postmodern Romances of Feminist Science Fiction', in Wolmark 1999: 230–8.

Woolf, Virginia (1977 [1929]), *A Room of One's Own* (London: Grafton Books).

—— (1983), *Between the Acts* (London: Grafton Books).

Wright, Terence (1988), *Theology and Literature* (Oxford: Blackwell).

Yaeger, Patricia (1988), *Honey-Mad Women: Emancipatory Strategies in Women's Writing* (New York: Columbia University Press).

Yorke, Liz (1991), *Impertinent Voices: Subversive Strategies in Contemporary Women's Poetry* (London: Routledge).

Index